The Complete

IDIOT'S

Pocket Reference to the

INTERNET

Neal Goldman

alpha
books

A Division of Macmillan Computer Publishing

201 West 103rd Street, Indianapolis, Indiana 46290 USA

For my mother-in-law Maria, who manages to have fun with her computer, despite the fact that it uses DOS.

Publisher

Marie Butler-Knight

Managing Editor

Elizabeth Keaffaber

Product Development Manager

Faithe Wempen

Acquisitions Manager

Barry Pruett

Manuscript Editor

San Dee Phillips

Book Designer

Barbara Kordesh

Indexer

Johnna Van Hoose

Production

Dan Caparo, Brad Chinn, Kim Cofer, Jennifer Eberhardt,
Erika Millen, Beth Rago, Bobbi Satterfield, Karen Walsh,
Robert Wolf

*Special Thanks to Martin Wyatt for ensuring the
technical accuracy of this book.*

Trademarks

Contents

Introduction

Unless you've been living in Tibet for the last two years searching for karmic truth, you've probably heard or read about the Internet, the "information superhighway," and how everyone will be connected by computer in the next five years and how our lives will be forever changed.

The Internet is a great service. With it, you can send electronic mail to millions of people, take part in discussion groups on thousands of topics from astrophysics to sports, and find tremendous volumes of information without ever leaving your computer. You can connect to university computers and government research computers, and download photographs, sound clips, and software of every type under the sun. You can even play interactive games with people all over the globe. Pick a topic, any topic, and you can probably find some discussion about it on the Internet.

How This Book Is Organized

This book is a concise reference for when you just want the instructions to perform a task without the big lecture. It gives you step-by-step instructions to all the kinds of activities you may want to do on the Internet. It is organized into several sections:

➤ "The Least You Need to Know," a section with general information you should know about before you plunge into the world of the Internet. Also included is a table of actions and the associated commands that you should look up in the A–Z reference.

➤ An A–Z command reference with step-by-step instructions on how to accomplish a task.

➤ An appendix showing you the basics of internet use through several popular online services.

➤ A listing of USENET newsgroups you can partici-
pate in on the Internet.

Since there are many different ways to access the
Internet, I will assume that you:

➤ Are using a direct terminal or some kind of modem
and a terminal program to connect to a commer-
cial Internet service provider.

➤ Are using the UNIX operating system as your way
of talking to the Internet. Unfortunately, most
service providers and Internet computers use
UNIX, which was designed by a bunch of brilliant
programmers who cared more about how few keys
they had to type than how easy it was to use.
Okay, with that attitude, maybe they weren't so
brilliant.

Conventions Used
in This Book

The following conventions are used to help you with
your voyage on the Internet:

What you type | The information you should
type appears in bold,
monospace text, such as:
Type **man**.

What you press | The keys you press appear as
keycaps, such as: Press `⏎Enter`.
For the example, press `Caps Lock`-`C`,
hold the Control key down as
you simultaneously type the
C key.

What you see | Information that you see
on-screen | on-screen appears in
monospace text, such as: At
the archie> prompt, type Set
Pager.

| Making an on-screen selection | When you are asked to make an on-screen selection, such as: Pull down the **Go To** menu, the selection will appear in a different font (see Appendix for examples). |

There are some special notes in this book to help you.

Tips show the easiest way to perform some tasks.

Special hints and examples on how to use a particular Internet command.

Acknowledgments

I'd like to thank the many people who helped put this book together. First, Barry Pruett at Alpha Books and Debbie McBride at Brady Books, who made it possible for me to write it. Thanks to Faithe Wempen and the rest of the development and production staff at Alpha for indulging me during the production process and making it as easy as possible for me. The World service from Software Tool & Die provided me excellent Internet access. And special thanks to my family and friends who have stuck by me, no matter what.

The Least You Need to Know

Before you drive on the information superhighway, it wouldn't be fair if I didn't tell you about some of the road signs you'll see and some of the rules that people on the road expect you to follow. (Well, I could leave you stranded, but you wouldn't enjoy it.) These are things you will encounter regardless of what you do on the Internet.

Names and Addresses

Every computer and person on the Internet has a unique address, just like a post office address (assuming you don't have roommates). To find anything on the net, you need its address.

There are two types of addresses: *IP addresses* and *domain names*. IP addresses are numbers that uniquely identify the computer, such as 129.74.137.5. These numbers identify which network, subnetwork, and computer you want to access and are very easy to remember once you get the hang of it (NOT!). Luckily, you almost never need the IP address.

Usually, you will see a domain name, which looks like world.std.com. These are much easier to remember. The domain name is actually interpreted right to left (no, it wasn't invented by someone who spoke Hebrew), with the rightmost piece representing the Domain of the network the computer is hooked to. Domain represents the type or location of the computer. Reading to the left narrows the scope until you get a unique machine. The following table represents some typical zones. Three-letter Domains are within the U.S. Country codes are two letters. Currently, there is not a designation for the Twilight Zone.

Domain	Meaning
com	Commercial organizations
edu	Educational institutions
gov	Government organizations
int	International organizations
mil	Military sites
net	Network resources (networked organizations)
org	Miscellaneous
au	Country (Australia)
uk	Country (United Kingdom)
de	Country (Germany)

E-Mail Addresses

People also have addresses for e-mail. A person's e-mail address is their *user name* followed by an @ and the domain name of their computer. For example, president@whitehouse.gov. is President Clinton's e-mail address. Don't be too disappointed if he doesn't respond personally.

Many online services, such as Compuserve and America Online, allow their users to receive e-mail via the Internet. To send a message to someone on one of these services:

Service	How to Address an E-Mail
America Online	Add @aol.com to the America Online user name. For example, case@aol.com

Service	How to Address an E-Mail
Applelink	Add @applelink.apple.com to the Applelink user name. For example, spindler@applelink.apple.com
Compuserve	Take the Compuserve address, replace the comma with a period and add @compuserve.com. For example, 73631,155 turns into 73631.155@compuserve.com
GEnie	Add @genie.geis.com to the GEnie user name. For example, welch@genie.geis.com
MCI Mail	Remove the hyphen from the MCI Mail user number and then add @mcimail.com. For example, 343-1932 becomes 3431932@mcimail.com

Don't guess someone's e-mail address, particularly if you don't know their user name. You'll never get it right unless you are the Amazing Kreskin. There are too many ways that people choose their user names. Call them up and ask them or try some of the search utilities, such as fred, finger, or whois (see A–Z reference section).

Culture, Etiquette, and Social Norms in Cyberspace

This is the preachy section. I'll get on my soapbox now.

The Internet, like any collection of people, has its own culture, norms, and expectations about people who join the community. The "guidelines" or "style of use" is known as *Netiquette*.

The Internet tends to be a very open and friendly place, allowing substantial access to information without a lot of passwords and identification. Everyone is encouraged to join. Additionally, there is no class structure. All users are equal. There is no single system administrator to monitor and control behavior and no user has any more power to control the actions of another user than anyone else. Your reputation is represented only by your actions on the keyboard. Below are some suggestions for things to watch out for as you surf the Internet.

- ➤ **Never forget that there are people on the other end.** Even though you are using a computer to communicate, don't forget that other people are on the receiving end. Avoid personal attacks. Try not to type anything to others that you would not say to them in a room full of people.

- ➤ **Be brief and use descriptive subject headings in messages.** With millions of people on the Internet, there are many words floating around. Using descriptive Subject headings increases the likelihood of your message being read. Staying on topic and writing concisely makes reading your messages easier.

- ➤ **Remember your audience can't see body language.** Online, no one can see your body language or hear your tone of voice. Be careful with humor and sarcasm. You must be aware of the tone of your words. When in doubt, you can use *emoticons*. Remember, in cyberspace, no one can hear you scream.

Following these few rules will drastically reduce the likelihood of someone *"flaming"* you. Flames are nasty messages, usually with epithets about your family background, that people send in response to something they don't like. You shouldn't flame. It's unattractive.

Okay. I can get off my soapbox now. I feel much better.

Emoticons

Since most of us aren't Ernest Hemingway and can't
evoke great emotions with a few well-chosen words,
people on the Internet have created a set of smileys
known as emoticons. You might see a : -) in the middle
of a paragraph. Look at it sideways, and it's a smiley face.
Cute, huh? Add these to a message when you want to
put some emotion into a sentence. For example,

> Congratulations on your promotion! :-)

So many of these have been created that you may
wonder what other more productive things the creators
could be doing. Below is a list of some common
emoticons. Don't overuse (abuse) them, PLEASE!

Emoticon	Meaning
:-)	Grin
:-(	Sadness
:->	Smile
:-<	Frown
;-)	Wink
:-o	Shock
:'-(	Crying
:-&	Tongue tied
7:^]	Ronald Reagan
]:o_ 　|O = 　|_o=	Cow

Electronic Shorthand

Common phrases are also often shortened to save typing and to confuse beginners. Below are some common abbreviations.

Abbreviation	Meaning
BTW	By the way
FWIW	For what it's worth
IMO	In my opinion
IMHO	In my humble opinion
LOL	Laugh out loud
ROFL	Roll on the floor laughing
CUL	See you later
WRT	With respect to
TIA	Thanks in advance
TTFN	Ta-ta for now

Getting Help and Further Information

Somewhere during your Internet travels, you are going to want some more information about the commands below. You're thinking, "What? This book doesn't cover everything?" I'm afraid not. It just covers the basics. Besides, on the Internet, everything is constantly changing. That's good for us book writers, but it means that in between revisions of our books, you're going to need to know how to find more information.

Luckily, most commands and utilities under UNIX come with online help. On UNIX, you use the man command (for manual) to find help. To find manual information on a given topic:

1. At the UNIX prompt, type man.

2. Press the [Spacebar] and type the topic you want help on. For example, archie

3. Hit [↵Enter].

You will see something like:

```
SYNOPSIS
      gopher [-sb] [-t title] [-p path]
[hostname port]
```

Anything in [ ] is optional. Anything with a dash (-) is a switch that modifies the behavior of the command. Following the synopsis will be a complete description of what the command does and what the switches do.

Unfortunately, a lot of these help pages are written by the programmers who wrote the program, so they can sometime be obtuse. Ever met a programmer who can write well? Ever met a programmer?

Directories and Files

UNIX stores all files in a hierarchical directory (or folder if you're a Macphile) structure that starts at the *root* directory. To find a file, you need to know in what directory (or branch) within the hierarchy (also known as a tree) it resides. The *path* tells UNIX how to find the file. If you detected an arboreal theme here, you score two points. There are no picket fences, though.

A *full path name* begins with a slash (/), indicating the root and continues from there. For example, /usr/ read.me would mean the file read.me resides in the usr directory and the usr directory is in the root. In DOS, you use a backslash (\), however, in UNIX, you use a forward slash (/).

A *relative path name* does not start with a slash (/) and indicates that the path should start from the current working directory. See the commands pwd and cd to see how to determine your current working directory and change it, respectively.

When UNIX calls for a file name, you can use either full or relative paths. When in doubt, use the full path.

There are several shortcuts you can use in path names to save typing (remember, everything in UNIX has a shortcut). A period (.) is shorthand for the current directory, while two periods (..) means the parent of the current directory. A tilde (~) is a shortcut for your home directory, which is where you start when you first connect to your system. Typing cd .. would change your directory to the one above your current directory.

Command Reference

This section contains an alphabetical listing of various commands that you will need to navigate the Internet and work with UNIX. If you don't know the name of the command you need, look at Table 1 below for a list of common actions and the appropriate command.

Where to Look in the Command Reference

Below is a list of things you may want to do and what utilities to look under in the A-Z Reference part of this book that follows.

Table 1   Where Do I Go?

Action	Where to Look
Sending and receiving e-mail	pine or mail (pine is easier)
Reading Internet News (also known as USENET or BBS)	tin or rn (tin is easier)
Copying files from another computer on the Internet	ftp
Copying files from your Internet computer to your personal computer	sz
Converting binary files to include in e-mail messages	uuencode or uudecode
Finding files to download	archie

continues

Table 1   Continued

Action	Where to Look
Finding information on the Internet	gopher, wais, www
Remotely logging in to another computer on the Internet	telnet
Finding computers to login to	hytelnet
Editing a text file in UNIX	pico or vi (pico is easier)

UNIX is case sensitive. This means that Unix considers **ftp** to be different from **FTP**. Most Unix commands are lowercase, so the Caps Lock key is generally evil. If something doesn't work, make sure that you are typing the text exactly as you see it in the proper case.

archie

Helps you find files by name that are located on FTP servers.

Have you ever walked into one of the warehouse-type stores and wondered, "How am I going to find that widget I wanted?" Imagine if there were no signs or people to ask. That's what it's like trying to find the particular file you want on the Internet. archie (the program, not the comic book character) is a program that helps you search for files by name across thousands of FTP servers around the world. It lists several million files and provides descriptions of many of them.

There are a couple of ways of getting to archie: using an archie client provided with your Internet service or by telnetting to an archie server. If you have access to an archie client, you should generally use it. If not, you must telnet to a computer that has an archie available to you. There are some limitations to the archie client, but the only one that is noteworthy is the lack of the whatis feature (see "archie: Using whatis with archie" later in this section).

Each section that follows contains specific directions for both the archie client and server, but in general, to connect to archie:

archie: Getting to archie with E-Mail

If you're so busy that you don't want to tie up your computer with an archie request, you can send e-mail to archie with the commands you want to do. archie will then process them at its leisure (as much leisure as an inanimate object is allowed to have) and send you back a response. To do this:

1. Start your mail utility (see *pine* or *mail*).

2. Address a message to: **archie@*archieserver*.**

Substitute the server you want to use for *archieserver* in step 2. For example, you might address the message to **archie.rutgers.edu**.

3. Type **archie request** as the subject of the message.

4. In the message body, type the commands that you want as if you were using the Telnet method.

archie: Initiating a File Search

Client Method:

1. At the UNIX prompt, type **archie**.

2. Press the ⟨ Spacebar ⟩ and type the name of the file you want to find.

For example, type **archie pkunzip.exe**.

3. Press ⟨↵Enter⟩.

The file name must be the exact name as it will be found on the FTP server, including the correct case of the letters (upper and lower). This is the fastest method of searching, but archie will only find exact matches using this method.

Telnet Method:

1. At the UNIX prompt, type **telnet**.

2. Press ⟨ Spacebar ⟩ and type the address of the archie server to which you want to connect.

For example, type **telnet archie.rutgers.edu**.

3. At the login: prompt, type **archie** and press ⟨↵Enter⟩.

4. At the archie> prompt, type **find**.

5. Press ⟨ Spacebar ⟩ and then type the name of the file you want to find.

For example, type **find pkunzip.exe**.

6. Press ⏎Enter. A list of files appears.

7. Type **quit** and press ⏎Enter to close the telnet connection and return to your host.

The find command is most common (in newer versions of archie), but you may encounter the prog command.

For either method, if there is a match, you will see the following kind of output.

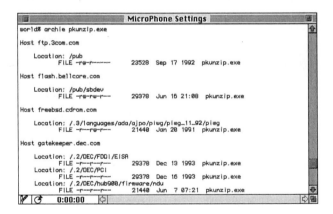

These list FTP servers (the hosts) and the directories that have the file. Now flip to the FTP section of this book to figure out how to bring the file back alive.

Following is a list of some archie servers you can telnet to. Choose the one that is closest to you to cut down network traffic.

Address	Location
archie.au	Australia
archie.uqam.ca	Canada
archie.doc.ic.ac.uk	United Kingdom
archie.unl.edu	USA (Nebraska)
archie.internic.net	USA (New Jersey)
archie.rutgers.edu	USA (New Jersey)
archie.ans.net	USA (New York)
archie.sura.net	USA (Maryland)

To find the latest list of archie servers the world over, send an e-mail (see *pine*, page 71 or *mail*, page 53) to **archie@archie.mcgill.ca**. In the body of the message, type the word **servers**. The server will automatically send you back a complete list of archie servers.

Some archie servers can get very crowded and limit the time that you can access them. Very unfriendly, but true. Some deny anyone access between 8:00 a.m. and 8:00 p.m. So you may have to wait or try other methods of archie access.

archie: Limiting How Long to Look

If you search for a common file name, such as read.me, your search could go on as long as the search for the Lock Ness monster. archie lets you limit the number of matches it finds before it stops searching.

archie Client Method:

1. Type **archie**.

2. Press ⌐ Spacebar ⌐, and then type **-m** followed by the number of files it should find before stopping.

For example, **-m10** will stop archie after it has found 10 files that match the criteria.

3. Continue with the instructions for the rest of your search.

Telnet Method:

1. Connect to the Telnet site (steps 1–3 of the Telnet procedure listed under "archie: Initiating a File Search").

2. At the archie> prompt, type **set maxhits**.

3. Press ⌐ Spacebar ⌐ and enter the number of files you want to match before stopping.

4. Press ⌐Enter⌐.

5. Continue with the rest of the steps of your search.

archie: Searching for Nonexact Names

Usually, you don't know the exact name and case of the file you are looking for. People name things most obscurely at times, particularly in the DOS world where there is an eight characters limit. archie lets you search for files if you only know a piece of the name. When you do this, you may get something you don't expect as well as the files you do. However, isn't surprise a spice of life?

There are three types of nonexact matching: sub, subcase, and regular expressions (regex).

➤ **Sub method** searches for a substring anywhere in the file name, not case sensitive. If searching for 'zip', for instance, archie would find ZIP.com, pkZip.exe, and unzip.dat. This is generally the preferred method.

➤ **Subcase method** also searches for a substring anywhere in the file name, but the case counts. So z and Z are considered different.

➤ **Regular expressions** (regex) allow you to define *wild cards* and patterns of characters to search for, such as "look for any files that start with numbers in their name". Regular expressions can get extremely complex. Of course, if you know how to calculate pi to 10 digits, you're all set.

Decide which method you want and then go for it.

Client Method:

1. At the UNIX prompt, type **archie**.

2. Press ⬚ Spacebar ⬚, then type one of the following:

    -s if you want the sub method.

    -c if you want the subcase method.

    -r if you want the regex method.

3. Press ⬚ Spacebar ⬚ and type the characters that you want to look for in the file name.

4. Press ⬚Enter⬚. A list of files will eventually appear.

For example, to search for files containing zip, type
archie -s zip.

Telnet Method:

1. At the UNIX prompt, type **telnet**.

2. Press [Spacebar] and type the archie server address.

3. At the login: prompt, type **archie** and press [⏎Enter].

4. At the archie> prompt, type **set search**.

5. Press [Spacebar] and type one of the following:

   sub if you want the sub method.

   subcase if you want the subcase method.

   regex if you want the regex method.

6. Press [⏎Enter].

7. At the archie> prompt, type **find**.

8. Press [Spacebar] and type the characters that you want to look for in the file name.

9. Press [⏎Enter]. A list of files will appear.

10. Type **quit** and press [⏎Enter] to close the Telnet connection and return to your host.

The find command is most common (in newer versions of archie), but you may encounter the prog command.

For any method, if there is a match, you will see the following kind of output.

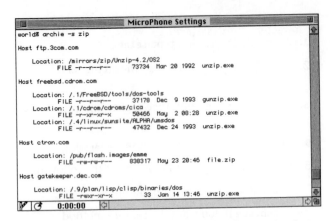

```
                   MicroPhone Settings
world% archie -s zip

Host ftp.3com.com

    Location: /mirrors/zip/Unzip-4.2/OS2
            FILE -r--r--r--     73734  Mar 20 1992  unzip.exe

Host freebsd.cdrom.com

    Location: /.1/FreeBSD/tools/dos-tools
            FILE -r--r--r--     37169  Dec  9 1993  gunzip.exe
    Location: /.1/cdrom/cdroms/cica
            FILE -r--xr-xr-x    50466  May  2 08:28  unzip.exe
    Location: /.4/linux/sunsite/ALPHA/umsdos
            FILE -r--r--r--     47432  Dec 24 1993  unzip.exe

Host ctron.com

    Location: /pub/flash.images/emme
            FILE -rw-rw-r--    838317  May 23 20:46  file.zip

Host gatekeeper.dec.com

    Location: /.9/plan/lisp/clisp/binaries/dos
            FILE -rwxr-xr-x       33  Jan 14 13:46  unzip.exe

   0:00:00
```

These list FTP servers (the host) and the directories that
have the file. Note that zip appears in different places in
different files. You need to look at the results and decide
which of these files might be the one you want.

archie: Using Regular Expressions in Searches

Warning! This section is not for the faint of heart.
Regular expressions are powerful search mechanisms,
but they are complex. These notes are for reference only.

Regular expressions allow sophisticated pattern matching to find file names. The string that contains the
regular expression is the *pattern*. In regular expressions,
certain characters take on special meaning to match sets
of characters, rather than an individual alphabetic
character.

The following table defines the special characters and
their meanings within regular expressions.

Character	Description
.	The period (.) matches any character. For example, the pattern .... would match any four characters in the string.

Character	Description
^	A caret (^) at the beginning of a pattern requires that the pattern occur at the beginning of the string. For example **^zip** would match zip.exe, but not pkzip.exe.
$	A dollar sign ($) at the end of the pattern means that a match will occur only if the pattern occurs at the end of the string. For example **exe$** would match zip.exe, but not execute.arc.
[x]	The brackets contain single characters to match within the string. **h[au]t** would match hut and hat, but not hit. A ^ at the beginning of the set (such as **[^abc]**) means to match any *except* those enclosed in the brackets. A - indicates a span of characters (**[a-z]** would match any character in the range a to z). To match a], place it first in the list (**[]xyz]**).
*	Match zero or more occurences of the immediately preceding expression. For example, **[a-z]*** matches zero or more occurences of a lowercase letter.
\	Using a \ preceding a special character makes it nonspecial. So **a\$b** would match the string a$b.
1\{m,n\}	The most complex of all. Match between m and n occurrences of the preceding regular expression. m and n must be between 0 and 255. For example, the pattern **x[a-f]\{2,4\}** would match a string with x followed by at least two, but at most four letters in the range a–f. The ,n is optional.

archie: Using whatis with archie

If during a search, you see an interesting file name in
your list, but you don't know what it is, the whatis
command may help you. archie keeps a descriptive
index of some of the files it knows about and you can
search it. Only files that have had descriptions entered
by humans will be in the index.

There is no archie client method of using whatis.

Telnet Method:

1. Connect to the Telnet site (steps 1–3 of the Telnet
   procedure listed under "archie: Getting to archie").

2. At the archie> prompt, type **whatis**.

3. Press (Spacebar) and type the name of the file
   you want to know about.

4. Continue with the rest of your searching.

If you typed **whatis zip**, you would see the following
response:

```
archie> whatis zip

unzip                          Unbundles ZIP files

unzip_gs                       UnZip for Unix
```

Notice that many of the zip files, such as pkzip.exe,
found in searches are not listed. With whatis, you are at
the whim of the archive managers who type these things
in.

archie: Working with Large File Lists

If your list is very large, it may fly by on your screen
before you get a chance to write down the host and
directory that contains the file. Each search method has
a way that you can slow down the scrolling or save the
output to a file for later viewing.

To use the switches in the archie client column:

1. Type **archie**.

2. Press (Spacebar), and then type the switch in the column.

3. Continue with the instructions for the rest of your search.

To use the switches in the Telnet column:

1. Connect to the Telnet site (steps 1–3 of the Telnet procedure listed under "archie: Getting to archie").

2. Press (Spacebar) and type the command from the column.

3. Continue with the rest of the steps of your search.

You can repeat step 2 as many times as necessary before going to step 3.

cat

Enables you to view a text file.

It would be nice if the way to view the contents of a file was simple to remember, like view or type. Sorry. The command is cat, which means "concatenate and display." Simple, huh? With it, you can actually combine files as well as displaying them.

To view a text file:

1. Type **cat**.

2. Press the (Spacebar).

3. Type the name of the file you want to view.

4. Press ⏎Enter.

For example, type `cat read.me`.

Cat does not pause as it displays the file. If the output goes by too quickly, look at the more and pg commands to find out how to display a file page by page.

cat: Combining Two Files Together

cat also allows you to combine several files together and create a file that contains them all. You will find this useful if someone has split up a large text file to e-mail it to you, for example.

1. Type **cat**.

2. Press the ⬚ Spacebar ⬚ and type the name of the first file you want to combine.

3. Press the ⬚ Spacebar ⬚ and type the name of the second file you want to combine.

4. Press the ⬚ Spacebar ⬚ and type a >.

5. Press the ⬚ Spacebar ⬚ and type the name of the file you want to create.

6. Press ⬚Enter⬚.

Let's say you have two files, cleverly named file1 and file2. To combine them into a new file called file3, you would type `cat file1 file2 > file3`. The > symbol tells UNIX to redirect the output from the screen to a file.

cat: Viewing a Text File with Line Numbers

If you want to see the output with a line number preceding each line of text:

1. Type **cat**.

2. Press the [Spacebar] and type **-n**.

3. Press the [Spacebar] and type the name of the file you want to view.

4. Press [⏎Enter].

For example, type **cat -n read.me**.

cd

Changes the current working directory on the UNIX system.

As you navigate around the Internet, you will invariably end up in a directory and want to change to another one to see what's there. You can always use full pathnames, but your fingers will eventually ache.

To change your current working directory to another one:

1. Type **cd**.

2. Press [Spacebar].

3. Type the path name of directory where you want to go.

See "The Least You Need to Know" at the beginning of this book for a discussion of paths.

4. Press [⏎Enter].

Try This!

For example, if you are currently in the /usr directory and want to go to the usr1 directory that is underneath the /usr directory, you would type **cd /usr/ usr1**. You can cheat and use the relative path name, by typing **cd usr1**.

Going to Your Home Directory

To quickly go to your home directory (no, you can't just click your heels and say, "there's no place like home"):

1. Type **cd**.

2. Press the [Spacebar] and type a / (slash).

3. Press [↵Enter].

cd: Moving Up One Directory Level

To go back one level in your directory tree:

1. Type **cd**.

2. Press [Spacebar] and type two dots (..).

3. Press [↵Enter].

cp

Copies files from one place to another in UNIX.

You'd think that to copy files, you'd type copy as your command. Guess again. This is UNIX, nothing is as it seems.

To copy one file to another:

1. Type **cp**.

2. Press [Spacebar] and type the name of the file to copy.

3. Press [Spacebar] and type the name for the copy.

4. Press ⏎Enter.

> # Try This!
>
> For example, typing `cp read.me readme.first`
> would copy the file `read.me` to a new file called
> readme.first.

Warning! The `cp` command assumes you know what
you are doing. UNIX has been called "user hostile" and
here is a case. If you type `copy t.txt x.txt` and `x.txt`
already exists, `cp` will gladly overwrite it with `t.txt` and
not inform you. This is generally considered to be bad.
To avoid this, use the `-i` switch (for inquire) before you
type the name of the file to copy to cause `cp` to ask
before overwriting. You may think it should work this
way by default, but it doesn't.

cp: Copying a File to Another Directory

If you want to create an extra copy of a file, but you
want it in another directory:

1. Type `cp`.

2. Press ⎵Spacebar⎵ and type the name of the
original file you want to copy.

3. Press ⎵Spacebar⎵ and type the name of the
directory where you want the copy to be.

4. (Optional) Type a new file name for the copy.

5. Press ⏎Enter.

If you skip step 4, the copy will have the same name as
the original.

cp: Copying Multiple Files to Another Directory

You can copy multiple files that have the same beginning part of the name with one command. For example,
if you have 12 files named chap01.txt through

chap12.txt, you can copy them all at once. To do this, use wild cards, such as ***** and **?**. The ***** stands for "zero or more characters," while the **?** stands for a single character. To do this:

1. Type **cp**.

2. Press [Spacebar] and type the wild-card specification of the files you want to copy.

3. Press [Spacebar] and type the name of the directory where you want the files to go.

4. Press [↵Enter].

Try This!

To copy 12 files named chap01.txt through chap12.txt to the /backup directory, you would type either **cp chap*.txt /backup** or **cp chap??.txt /backup**.

find

Searches for a file when you know part of its name.

Ever misplace your keys? It's even easier to misplace files. Sometimes, you forget where you put the file, other times, you just mistype something and the file goes somewhere you don't expect. If you know part of its name, you can find the file by:

1. Type **find**.

2. Press [Spacebar] and type the path name of where you want to search. To search from root on down the directory tree, type **/**.

3. Press [Spacebar] and type **-name**.

4. Press [Spacebar] and type the name of the file you are looking for in quotes (**" "**).

5. Press [Spacebar] and type **-print**.

6. Press [↵Enter].

For example, to find the file t.txt (very memorable file name—no wonder I lost it), in any directories in the current directory or below, you would type **find . -name "t.txt" -print**. If you want to start the search from the root, use a slash (/) instead of the period (.).

finger

Finds someone's address on the Internet.

finger will help you find a person, and their specific e-mail address, but you generally have to know the name of the machine they work on. finger can also be used to find what people are currently logged into a particular machine.

Rule #1 in finding someone's e-mail address: Call them up first and ask them! Searching for an e-mail address on the Internet is usually a futile and frustrating effort. Don't waste your time unless you have to. Perhaps you're trying to find someone who owes you money, or someone who doesn't speak your language.

finger: Finding a Person if You Have Their Domain Name

If you know the domain name, but you don't know their user name, but you know either something of their user name or their "real life" name:

1. Type **finger**.

2. Press [Spacebar] and type the person's name.

3. Press [Spacebar].

4. Type @ followed by the domain name.

5. Press ⏎Enter.

For example, type **finger steve@inmet.com**.

You will see a list of people from whom you can (hopefully) choose. For example, if you were looking for a Steve at the machine inmet.com, you would see the following:

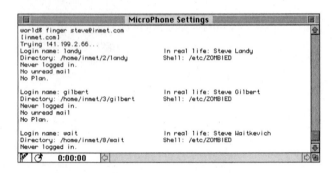

finger: Finding the People Currently Logged In to a Machine

1. Type **finger**.

2. Press ⟨ Spacebar ⟩ and type @ followed by the machine name. For example, **@inmet.com**.

3. Press ⏎Enter.

fred

Another way to find someone's address on the Internet.

fred (not the one married to Wilma) is a program that provides access to a set of "white page" directories of about 50 companies. If who you want to look for is part of these directories, great. Otherwise, keep looking (see finger and whois). To get to `fred`, you need to telnet (see the `telnet` command for more information) to `wp.psi.com` or `wp1.psi.com`. By the way, `fred` is named for FRont End to Directories, yet another testament to obscure origins of UNIX commands.

Rule #1 in finding someone's e-mail address: Call them up first and ask them! Searching for an e-mail address on the Internet is usually a futile and frustrating effort. Don't waste your time unless you have to.

To find a person using `fred`:

1. Type **telnet wp.psi.com** (or **wp1.psi.com**).

2. Press ⏎Enter.

3. When the `login:` prompt appears, type **fred** and press ⏎Enter.

4. At the `fred>` prompt, type **whois**.

5. Press ⎵Spacebar and type the name of the person you want to find.

6. Press ⏎Enter.

Beware! fred is flaky and not the most reliable program you will find.

Tip

To find what organizations are listed, at the `fred>` prompt, type **whois -org *** and press ⏎Enter. If you want to narrow your person search to a particular organization, such as Apple, between steps 5 and 6, you would type **-org Apple***.

ftp

Transferring files around the Internet.

ftp is one of the big four commands on the Internet.
With gigabytes of stuff out there for the taking, ftp is
the way to take it. *FTP* stands for File Transfer Protocol
(original, huh?) and is the means by which computers
talk to each other as they transfer files. It is also, in small
letters, the name of the program that lets you transfer
files. Like all good computer acronyms, you can use FTP
as a noun, verb, or adjective when you want to talk
nerdspeak (as in "I ftp'ed to the sumex FTP site and then
managed to crash ftp").

Many FTP sites are referred to as *anonymous,* not
because they have anything to hide, but because that
is the user name that the site has set up for general
public access.

ftp: Connecting to an FTP Site

To transfer files from an FTP site, you must establish a
connection to it. To do this:

1. At the UNIX prompt, type **ftp**.

2. Press ⌐ Spacebar ⌐ and type the host name of
   the FTP site to which you want to connect (for
   example, **internic.net**).

3. Press ⌐Enter⌐.

4. At the user name prompt (usually Name:), type
   anonymous.

5. Press ⌐Enter⌐.

6. If you are prompted for a password, type your
   e-mail address (for example, **ngoldman@
   world.std.com**).

In step 6, you can type anything, but site managers use your e-mail address to track who uses the system. Not all FTP sites require a password.

You should now be connected to the FTP server.

> If you are already in `ftp` (namely you are at the `ftp>` prompt), to open a connection to a different FTP site, type **open** for step 1 instead of **ftp** and proceed with the rest of the steps.

```
                     MicroPhone Settings
world% ftp internic.net
Connected to internic.net.
220-*****Welcome to the InterNIC Registration Host  *****
     *****Login with username "anonymous"
     *****You may change directories to the following:
     policy          - Registration Policies
     templates       - Registration Templates
     netinfo         - NIC Information Files
     domain          - Root Domain Zone Files
220 And more!
Name (internic.net:ngoldman): anonymous
331 Guest login ok, send your email address as password.
Password:
230 Guest login ok, access restrictions apply.
Remote system type is UNIX.
Using binary mode to transfer files.
ftp> █
        0:00:00
```

ftp: Determining File Type

If you run a Macintosh, downloading some nice DOS utility isn't going to do you much good. Figuring out what type a file is beforehand will prevent you from wasting time downloading useless files. Fortunately, there are conventions for naming files to make it easy to identify file types just by looking at their name.

There are many ways of encoding and compressing files to make them smaller and easier to transfer over the Internet. Once you download a file, you must run the appropriate utility to decode or uncompress the file to use it. You can download these utilities from various sites over the Internet.

Try This!

Sometimes, a file can have two attributes to them. For example, if you saw the file name deluxe-solitaire.sit.hqx, you would think that it might contain a solitaire game that has first been compressed with the Stuffit utility (the .sit part) and had then been encoded with the BinHex utility (the .hqx part). To see the real file, you need to download it to your Mac, un-BinHex it, and then UnStuffit using those utilities on your Mac. Got that?

The following table contains extensions and the utilities you will need.

File extension	Operating System	Utility File Type
.arc	DOS	ARC
.cpt	Macintosh	Compact Pro
.exe	DOS	DOS executable
.gif	Any	Graphics Interchange file
.gz	UNIX	Gzip
.hqx	Macintosh	BinHex 4.0
.jpg	Any	Graphics file (JPEG)
.lzh	DOS	LHArc
.mpg	Any	video file (MPEG)
.pict	Macintosh	Graphic file
.sea	Macintosh	Self Extracting Archive
.sit	Macintosh	Stuffit
.tar	UNIX	Tar
.tif	Any	Graphics File (TIFF)
.txt	Any	Text File

File extension	Operating System	Utility File Type
.uu	UNIX	Uudecode
.Z	UNIX	Uncompress
.z	Unix	Unpack
.zip	DOS	PKzip
.zoo	Unix	Zoo

ftp: Downloading a File

To download a file:

1. At the ftp> prompt, type **get**.

2. Press [Spacebar] and type the name of the file you want to download.

3. (Optional) Press [Spacebar] and type the name you want the file to have on your computer.

4. Press [↵Enter].

Important! ftp will copy the file to the computer that is running ftp. If you are using a modem to dial in to a service provider, the file will end up on their computer in your current directory. To copy the file from the service provider to your computer, use the sz command.

You can combine the get and sz command to bypass having to copy the file to the service provider's computer. To do this, type the get command as follows: **get** *filename* "|sz -", including the quotes. If you want to change the output file name as well, type: **get** *filename* "|ONAME=*filename* sz -".

36 *Command Reference*

ftp: Downloading Multiple Files with ftp

To copy more than one file at a time using wild cards:

1. At the ftp> prompt, type **mget**.

2. Press [Spacebar] and type the file names you want to copy. For example, ***.txt** or **choc***.

3. Press [⏎Enter].

4. At the confirmation prompt for each file, press [y] if you want to download, or [n] if you don't.

If you don't want to be prompted, type **prompt** and press [⏎Enter] at the ftp> prompt before step 1.

ftp: Navigating Directories

Sitting at the ftp> prompt and wondering what this site has to offer? Perhaps it contains a program that will help you pick winning lottery numbers. How do you find out? Well, FTP sites look just like directory structures, and you navigate them the same way .

Many FTP sites also provide three files that tell you what files are available. The README file is usually short and will describe what kind of files are available in the site or directory. The INDEX file will list files with brief descriptions of them. Sometimes, there is a file called ls-lR that contains a comprehensive directory listing of the FTP site. These files are often enormous, but they let you peruse the file listing using an editor rather than sitting in FTP. See "Downloading Files" for instructions to be able to read these files.

Remember files names are case sensitive in `ftp` as well as in UNIX. You must type the letters and also their case correctly. It's a pain, but who said UNIX was easy?

To find out what directory you are in currently:

1. At the `ftp>` prompt, type **pwd**.

2. Press (⏎Enter).

To find out what files are located in the current directory:

1. At the `ftp>` prompt, type **ls**.

2. Press (⏎Enter).

You will see something that looks like this:

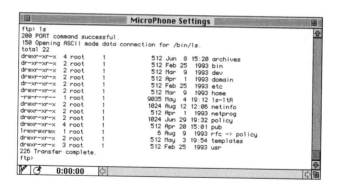

Notice the first letter in each line of the directory listing. If it is a d, then the file is a directory. A hyphen (-) indicates a file.

To see a directory listing of the current directory that stops at each page:

1. At the `ftp>` prompt, type **ls ¦more**. Make sure you don't put a space between the ¦ and the **more**.

2. Press ⏎Enter.

3. At each pause, press ⎵Spacebar⎵ to see the next page or press q to stop.

To change to a new current directory on the FTP host:

1. At the ftp> prompt, type **cd**.

2. Press ⎵Spacebar⎵.

3. Type the path name of directory where you want to go.

4. Press ⏎Enter.

See the section "The Least You Need to Know" at the beginning of this book for a discussion of paths.

You can move up one directory level by using the command **cdup**, or by typing **cd** followed by two periods (**..**).

Sometimes, you see a directory listing that looks like:

```
lrwxrwxrwx  1 root    daemon   6 Aug 12  1992
U.S.Supreme.Court -> hermes
drwxr-xr-x  8 uucp    daemon 512 Aug  1 18:04 hermes
```

The -> indicates a link or an alias (not like those on FBI wanted posters). Typing either **cd U.S.Supreme.Court**, or **cd hermes**, will take you to the hermes directory.

ftp: Quitting an ftp Session

As much fun as FTP is, at some point, you are probably going to want to stop. You can either close a specific connection and open a new one, or you can quit ftp.

To close a connection:

1. At the ftp> prompt, type **close**.

2. Press ⏎Enter.

You will remain in ftp. To open a new connection, see Connecting to an FTP site.

To quit ftp:

1. At the ftp> prompt, type **quit**.

2. Press ⏎Enter.

ftp: Setting the Mode of the Transfer

The ftp program can copy files in two modes: *ASCII* (text) or *binary* (everything else). Generally, you want to transfer files in binary mode, but if you know a file is text, you should change the mode to ASCII.

To change the mode to ASCII:

1. At the ftp> prompt, type **ascii**.

2. Press ⏎Enter.

ftp will respond with the message Type set to A.

To change the mode to binary.

1. At the ftp> prompt, type **binary**.

2. Press ⏎Enter.

ftp will respond with the message Type set to I. I? Why not B? Better not to question. The I stands for image.

ftp: Specifying a Directory on Your Client Computer

If you want to change the directory where the files will be copied when you download them:

1. At the ftp> prompt, type **lcd**.

2. Press ⎵Spacebar and type the directory name where you want files to be copied.

3. Press ⏎Enter.

ftp: Uploading a File Using ftp

You must have upload permission on the FTP site to do this! To upload a file:

1. At the `ftp>` prompt, type **put**.

2. Press ⌷ Spacebar ⌷ and type the name of the file you want to upload.

3. (Optional) Press ⌷ Spacebar ⌷ and type the name you want the file to have on the FTP site.

4. Press ⌷↵Enter⌷.

gopher

Navigate Internet services using a menu system.

Frustrated that you don't know where to look for things on the Internet? Or what may be out there? Gopher is a furry, little rodent (okay, it's really a program) that knows where things are and how to go for them. It presents what it knows in a series of menus and all you need to do is select the one you want and press ⌷↵Enter⌷. Nothing simpler.

But (and there's always a but on the Internet), gopher only knows about things that people have told it. While it covers a lot of ground, it's not comprehensive by any stretch of the imagination, even Stephen Hawking's.

Gopher is actually a decentralized system of gopher servers around the world, each of which contains links to menus and items in other servers. While this makes it easy to find things on different machines, it also means that there is no organization to gopher menus. You also may find that different gopher servers use slight command variations.

To start gopher, if your service provider supplies a gopher client:

1. Type **gopher**.

2. Press ⌷↵Enter⌷.

If your service provider doesn't supply a gopher client, *complain*. It's trivial for them to set one up and it will speed up your access. In the meantime, you need to telnet to a gopher site (see telnet):

1. Type **telnet**.

2. Press [Spacebar] and type the name of the gopher site (try consultant.micro.umn.edu).

3. Press [⏎Enter].

4. At the login: prompt, type **gopher**.

5. Press [⏎Enter].

After either method, you should see a screen that looks like this:

Notice that in the lower right corner is a 1/2. This means that it's page 1 of 2 pages.

The granddaddy of all gopher sites is the University of Minnesota, originator of the gopher program. The fact that their mascot is the Golden Gopher was meaningless to their naming this program. Other gopher sites to telnet to:

continues

continued

Host name	IP#	Login	Area
ux1.cso.uiuc.edu	128.174.5.59	gopher	North America Illinois
panda.uiowa.edu	128.255.40.201	panda	North America Iowa
gopher.msu.edu	35.8.2.61	gopher	North America Michigan
gopher.ebone.net	192.36.125.2	gopher	Europe

gopher: Figuring Out What an Item Is

Each menu item often contains an indicator as to what it is. A slash (/) means that choosing it will bring you to another menu. A period (.) means that the item is a file. A <TEL> indicates a telnet site and choosing it will telnet you there. <?> will let you search for something. To get further information on an item:

1. Type =.

   You will see something that looks like:

   ```
   Name=Other Gopher and Information Servers
   Type=1
   Port=70
   Path=1/Other Gopher and Information Servers
   Host=gopher.tc.umn.edu
   ```

2. Press ⏎Enter to return to the menu.

The following table contains the list of types and what they mean.

Type	What It Means
0	A file.
1	A directory. One of these will take you to other menus.
2	CSO (qi) phone-book server.
4	A BinHexed Macintosh file.
5	A DOS binary archive of some sort.
6	A UNIX uuencoded file.
7	An Index-Search server. Same as <?>.
8	A text-based telnet session.
9	A binary file! Client must read until the connection closes.
T	TN3270 connection.
s	Sound type. Data stream is a mulaw sound.
g	GIF type.
M	MIME type. Item contains MIME data.
h	html type.
I	Image type.
i	"inline" text type.

gopher: Menuing

Navigating through gopherspace is very simple.

To choose an item:

    1A. Use the ⬆ or ⬇ to move the pointer (—>) to the item you want.

       OR

    1B. Type the number of the item you want.

2. Press `↵Enter`.

Following is a table with commands and what they do.
You do not have to press `↵Enter` for each one.

Key to Press	Action
`Spacebar` (or `>`, `+`, `PgDn`)	View the next page of the menu.
`b` (or `<`, `-`, `PgUp`)	View the previous page of the menu.
`u` (or `←`)	Go back to the previous menu.
`m`	Go back to the main menu.
`q`	Quit gopher.
`/`	Search for a string in the menu.
`n`	Search for the next match.

gopher: Saving Files

Gopher lets you easily navigate to a file, and it's equally
easy to save a file. When you finish reading a text file, or
you type = to find out its type, you will see the following
prompt:

```
Press <RETURN> to continue, <m> to
mail, <s> to save, or <p> to print:
```

Alternatively, if you see an item that ends with a period
(.) indicating that it is a file, select it using the `↑` and `↓`
and follow the directions below.

To save the file:

1. Type **s**.

2. At the Enter save file name: prompt, type the
name you want the file to be saved as.

3. Press ‹┘Enter›.

This will copy the file to your home directory. If you use a modem to access the Internet, you will need to use the sz command to transfer the file to your personal computer.

If you want to download directly to your personal computer, select a file with the up and down arrow keys and type **D** (not d!), instead of s. A dialog box will appear asking you to choose a transfer protocol. Type the number corresponding to the one you want, and press ‹┘Enter›.

If you have telnetted to gopher, you must do this. You can't save from a telnet site.

gopher: Searching Using Veronica

With so many gopher servers out there, it can be difficult to find things you want without wasting a lot of time navigating through places you don't want. Veronica will rescue you. The creators claim the name had nothing to do with archie. I'm sure they came up with Very Easy Rodent-Oriented Net-wide Index to Computerized Archives totally independently.

Veronica lets you search using keywords across gopherspace. You type the keyword you want and Veronica returns with a gopher menu containing items that match the keyword.

To use Veronica:

1. You need to find a menu item in gopher that looks like:

       18. Other Gopher and Information Servers/

2. Select that menu item using the ‹↑› and ‹↓› and press ‹┘Enter›. You will see:

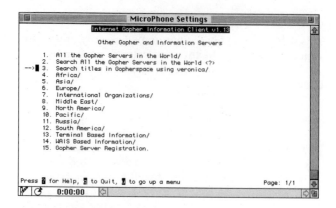

3. Select the item Search titles in Gopherspace
   with veronica/.

4. Press [↵Enter].

5. Select one of the options to search gopherspace by
   selecting one of the many servers.

6. Press [↵Enter].

7. At the Words to search for: prompt, type the
   keyword you want.

8. Press [↵Enter].

Below is a sample picture where the search is for Jughead
(Jonzy's Universal Gopher Hierarchy Excavation And
Display).

gopher: Setting Bookmarks

After navigating through many menus, you may find it difficult to remember how to get back to a particular place. Gopher lets you set up bookmarks which will quickly return to a location.

To set a bookmark on an item:

1. Select the item by using the ⬆ and ⬇.

2. Type **a**.

3. At the prompt for what to call the bookmark, press ⏎Enter to choose the default. You can choose to enter your own text to customize it.

To set a bookmark for the current menu:

1. Type **A**.

2. At the prompt for what to call the bookmark, press ⏎Enter to choose the default. You can choose to enter your own text to customize it.

To use a bookmark:

1. Type **v** to bring up the list of bookmarks.

2. Use the ⬆ and ⬇ to choose a bookmark.

3. Press ⏎Enter.

To delete a bookmark:

1. Type **v** to bring up the list of bookmarks.

2. Use the ⬆ and ⬇ to choose the bookmark to delete.

3. Type **d**.

4. Type **u** to get back to the previous menu.

grep

Searches for text in a file.

Grep is a great little utility if you know that somewhere on your disk is a file that contains your résumé and you just *can't* remember what the file name was. Of course, since grep is such a mnemonic name, you'll never have trouble remembering it. With grep, you specify the text and directories to search, and it will come back with the files that contain the text.

To find files by searching their text:

1. Type **grep**.

2. Press [Spacebar] and type the words you want to search for, enclosed in quotes (`""`).

3. Press [Spacebar] and type the file specification for the set of files you want to search.

4. Press [↵Enter].

For example, type **grep "job experience" *.doc**.

To find files by searching their text and the case of the text doesn't matter:

1. Type **grep**.

2. Press [Spacebar] and type **-i**.

3. Press [Spacebar] and type the words you want to search for, enclosed in quotes (`""`).

4. Press [Spacebar] and type the file specification for the set of files you want to search.

5. Press [↵Enter].

If it doesn't find anything, it just returns to the prompt.

For example, type **grep -i "job experience" *.doc**.

To find files and not display all the lines found in the file:

1. Type **grep**.

2. Press [Spacebar] and type **-l**.

3. Press [Spacebar] and type the words you want to search for, enclosed in quotes (**" "**).

4. Press [Spacebar] and type the file specification for the set of files you want to search.

5. Press [⏎Enter].

For example, type **grep -l "job experience"**
*.doc.

Grep is a powerful search mechanism and it can search for regular expressions as well as text (see regular expressions under Archie). It stands for the incredibly obvious Global Regular Expression and Print. With regular expressions, you can construct some very complex searches that are too techy to believe. If you want to explore regular expressions, type **man grep** at the UNIX prompt and learn more than you will ever want.

hytelnet

Finds cool places to telnet to.

Often, you find telnet sites by looking at other books (Alpha books are the best), through newsgroups, and by eavesdropping at your company's MIS department Christmas party. Or you can use hytelnet, a useful menu-based utility that lets you select telnet sites by category.

To use hytelnet:

1. Type **hytelnet**.

2. Press ⏎Enter. You will see the following:

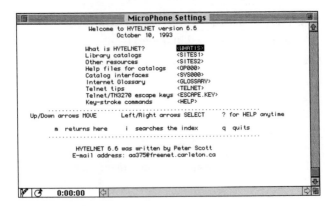

3. Use the ↑ and ↓ to select the item you want.

4. Press ⏎Enter.

5. Repeat steps 3 and 4 until you come to an item you want. You will eventually see something like this:

The top part of the listing will give you instructions as to how to telnet to the site, including instructions for specific login names or menu selections.

Hytelnet will sometimes give you the option of automatically telnetting for you. To do this, hit the ⏎Enter key.

If your service provider doesn't have hytelnet, never fear. There are several telnet sites that offer hytelnet for you. To remotely access hytelnet:

1. Type **telnet access.usask.ca**.
2. Press ⏎Enter.
3. At the login: prompt, type **hytelnet** and press ⏎Enter.

ls

List the files in a directory.

ls is the command that lists what files are in a particular directory. There are many switches that determine what kinds of information about files you see. I'll just show a few.

To list the files in the current directory (name only):

1. Type **ls**.
2. Press ⏎Enter.

If there are lots of files in the directory, you can list them a page at a time by adding ¦**more** to the end of any **ls** command. Remember, no space between the ¦ and the **more**.

To list the files in the current directory (including all information):

1. Type **ls**.
2. Press ⌷ Spacebar ⌷ and type **-l**.
3. Press ⌷Enter⌷.

You will see something like this:

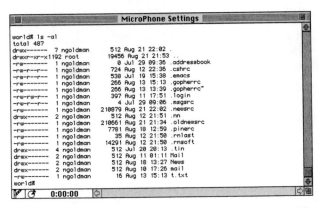

The first character tells whether the file is a directory (d) or a file (–). The next letters indicate the file access permissions for the owner, group, and world. The first number you can ignore. Next is the owner's name and group; following that is the size of the file, its date of creation and finally, its name.

To list all the files, including hidden ones, in the current directory:

1. Type **ls**.
2. Press ⌷ Spacebar ⌷ and type **-a**.
3. Press ⌷Enter⌷.

To list the files in another directory:

1. Type **ls**.
2. Press ⌷ Spacebar ⌷ and type the path name of the directory (see Directories and Files in the A–Z Introduction).
3. Press ⌷Enter⌷.

For example, typing `ls -al /usr/pub |more` would show the complete directory listing of all the files in the directory /usr/pub and page the output. Typing `ls *.txt` would show all the files that end with .txt in the current directory.

mail

Sends and receives electronic mail.

Everyone loves to get mail. No wonder e-mail is the most widely used feature of the Internet. It's cheap, easy, and much faster than the traditional letter. Many people think that e-mail will bring back the era of letter writing, albeit in a slightly different form.

The UNIX mail program comes with most UNIX systems. It's ugly, but it works. If you can use another program, such as pine (see *pine*), you should do so. Ask your system administrator for a favor.

Sometimes, the mail program is called `mailx`, or `Mail`. Try them until you find the one that's on your system.

mail: Deleting Messages

Deleting messages is an essential part of e-mail. Otherwise, you will never be able to keep track of the old and new.

To delete a message:

1. At the & prompt, type **d**.

2. (Optional) Press `Spacebar` and type the message number you want to delete.

If you don't specify a number, mail will delete the last message you read.

3. Press ⏎Enter.

Tip

If you accidentally delete a message, just undelete it.
Type **u** instead of **d** in step 1. The message will
reappear.

Try This!

For example, **d 3** would delete message 3. You can
also delete multiple messages at once. **d 4-8** would
delete messages 4 through 8.

mail: Forwarding a Message

To forward a message, you send a message and include
the other message in it.

To forward a message:

1. At either the UNIX prompt or the & prompt, type
   mail.

2. Press ⌷ Spacebar ⌷ and type the person's e-mail
   address to whom you want to forward a message.

3. (Optional) For multiple recipients, press
   ⌷ Spacebar ⌷ and type an additional address.

4. Press ⏎Enter.

5. At the Subject: prompt, type the subject of your
   message.

6. Press ⏎Enter.

7. Type ~f.

8. Press ⌷ Spacebar ⌷ and type the number of the
   message you want to forward.

9. Press ⏎Enter.

10. To finish, type a period (.) or press Ctrl-D and then press ⏎Enter.

On some systems, you will see a Cc: prompt after your message. If you want to carbon copy people, type their addresses and press ⏎Enter. Mail will respond with EOT (End of Text). Your message has been sent.

mail: Including a File in a Message

Rather than typing your message directly into mail, you may want to attach a file and send that instead. You can create the message using a text editor, rather than having to rely on mail's primitive editor. Or maybe you want to mail that list of lawyer jokes to your friend in California.

> **WARNING! WARNING!** Danger Will Robinson! You can only send text (ASCII) files using UNIX mail! You cannot send binary files without a special process (see *uuencode*). Use uuencode to convert a binary file to text. You then include it as part of the message and the recipient runs uudecode on the message to convert it back to binary (see *uudecode*).

To send a text file using mail:

1. At either the UNIX prompt or the & prompt, type **mail**.

2. Press ⌴Spacebar and type the e-mail address of the person to whom you want to send a message.

3. (Optional) For multiple recipients, press ⌴Spacebar and type an additional address.

Try This!

For example, to send a message to Alpha Books, you would use `mail fwempen@halcyon.com`.

4. Press ⏎Enter.

5. At the Subject: prompt, type the subject of your message.

6. Press ⏎Enter.

7. Type ~r.

8. Press ⎵Spacebar and type the name of the file you want to attach.

9. Press ⏎Enter.

10. To finish, type a period (.) or press Ctrl-D, and press ⏎Enter.

On some systems, you will see a Cc: prompt after your message. If you want to carbon copy people, type their addresses and press ⏎Enter.

mail: Quitting Mail

Mail is unusual for an Internet utility in that depending on how you exit, different things occur. All the actions you performed, such as deleting or moving messages, are buffered. These changes are only finalized when you quit. Also, mail will automatically save any messages you have read to a file called mbox. You can choose to have these things occur or not depending on which exit command you use.

To quit mail and have changes occur:

1. At the & prompt, type q.

2. Press ⏎Enter.

To quit mail and have no changes occur:

1. At the & prompt, type x.

2. Press ⏎Enter.

With this option, no messages are saved to mbox and no messages are deleted, including those you actually asked to be deleted.

If you want any read messages to remain in your mailbox, you can use the preserve command. Before you quit, type **pre**, followed by ⸢ Spacebar ⸥ and the number of the message you want to remain in your mailbox after you quit. Press ⸢↵Enter⸥.

mail: Reading Your E-Mail

To read your mail, you must start the mail program and view a list of messages you've received. Then you choose the message you want to read.

To see the list of messages you have:

1. Type **mail**. (You may have to try **mailx** or **Mail**).

2. Press ⸢↵Enter⸥.

If you have no messages, **mail** will display the message No mail for username, and quit back to the UNIX prompt. Username is your username. It's not as bad as it looks. Each line tells you the number of the message, who sent it to you, the date and time it came in, the size (number of lines/number of bytes) and the subject. The first character on the line tells you the message status:

N	New. Indicates that the message is new and has not been read yet.
U	Unread. You saw the message but didn't read it the last time you checked mail.
P	Preserved. You told mail not to remove this message automatically from the inbox by using the preserve command.
Space	You've read this message sometime during this mail session.
>	This message is the *current* message.

If you have so many messages that all the headers
don't fit on one screen, mail will pause after the first
20 or so. Type **z** and press ↵Enter to see the next
screenful of headers. Typing **-z** will show you the
previous screenful. Typing **h** and pressing ↵Enter will
show you the list from the beginning. To see the
headers for a specific set of messages, type **f** followed
by the numbers of the messages you want to see and
press ↵Enter. For example, **f 3-10** will show you the
headers for messages 3 through 10.

To read the current message:

1. If the message you want to read has the > in front
   of it, just press ↵Enter.

2. To continue reading your messages in sequence,
   continue to press ↵Enter.

To read a particular message:

1. At the & prompt, type the number of the message
   you want to read.

2. Press ↵Enter.

mail: Replying to a Message

Lots of messages deserve snappy comebacks. Mail will let
you reply directly to a message either to the original
sender or to both the sender and all the other recipients
of the message.

You'll soon discover that e-mail etiquette dictates that
you include the original message as the first part of your
message to remind the reader what the original said.
Usually, you only want to do this if the message was
short, otherwise you should paraphrase to keep the reply
concise.

To reply to a message:

1. At the & prompt, type **r**.

2. (Optional) Press [Spacebar] and type the number of the message to which you want to reply.

If you leave off the number in step 2, you will reply to the current (marked with a >) message.

3. Press [↵Enter]. Mail fills in the subject line as a response.

4. (Optional) To include the text of the message you are replying to, type ~m, a space, the message number, and press [↵Enter].

5. Type in the text of your reply.

Mail will not automatically wrap lines, so you must hit Enter approximately every 60 characters so the message will look good on the recipient's screen. The snap is up to you.

6. When finished, press [↵Enter], type a period (.) or press [Ctrl]-[D].

7. Press [↵Enter].

On some systems, you will see a Cc: prompt after your message. If you want to carbon copy people, type their addresses and press [↵Enter].

mail: Saving a Message to a File

If someone sends you the best joke you've ever read and you simply must keep it for posterity, you can save the message to a text file.

To save a message to a file:

1. At the & prompt, type **s**.

2. Press [Spacebar] and type the number of the message you want to save.

3. Press [Spacebar] and type the file name in which to save the message.

4. Press [↵Enter].

You can save multiple messages by including multiple message numbers in the command. For instance, **s 5-8 message.txt** would put messages 5 through 8 in the file message.txt.

mail: Sending a Message

Just like Mom used to say, you can't get any mail unless you send some out. Of course, you need to know the recipient's address (see E-mail addresses in the Introduction).

To send a message:

1. At either the UNIX prompt, or the & prompt, type **mail**.

2. Press [Spacebar] and type the recipient's e-mail address.

3. (Optional) For multiple recipients, press [Spacebar] and type an additional address.

4. Press [↵Enter].

For example, to send a message to Alpha Books, you would use **mail fwempen@halcyon.com**.

5. At the `Subject:` prompt, type the subject of your message.

6. Press ⏎Enter.

7. Type the text of your message.

Mail will not automatically wrap lines, so you must hit ⏎Enter approximately every 60 characters so the message will look good on the recipient's screen.

8. To finish, press ⏎Enter, then type a period (.) or press Ctrl-D and press ⏎Enter.

On some systems, you will see a `Cc:` prompt after your message. If you want to carbon copy people, type their addresses and press ⏎Enter. Mail will respond with EOT (End of Text). Your message has been sent.

If you want to cancel the sending of a message before you finish, Press Ctrl-C twice.

man

Gets help on a topic.

Many nice developers provide help on their Internet utilities. If you have questions about a particular command, or hear about a new utility on your service provider that you want to learn about, use the man command to see if there is help.

"man" stands for "manual"—it's not a reflection on one's gender.

Since these "man pages" are often written by UNIX programmers, be prepared for some terminology in the help that you've never heard of before. Rule of thumb: If you can't understand the terminology, you probably don't need to know about it. There are some very obscure options to some commands.

To get help on a topic:

1. Type **man**.

2. Press [Spacebar] and type the name of the topic you want help on.

3. Press [↵Enter].

mkdir

Makes a new directory.

Directories help you organize your files on your disk. Creating directories will make your disk as neat as your desk.

To make a new directory:

1. Type **mkdir**.

2. Press [Spacebar] and type the name you want the directory to make.

If you don't specify a full path name, mkdir will create a subdirectory in your current working directory (see *cd*).

For example, if your current working directory is /home and you type **mkdir test**, you would create the directory /home/test.

more

Views a text file with pauses for each screenful.

If a file is long, using the `cat` command to view it will cause the contents to fly by faster than you can read it (even if you've taken Evelyn Wood's speedreading class).

To view a file with pauses at each page:

1. Type **more**.

2. Press [Spacebar] and type the name of the file you want to view.

3. Press [↵Enter].

More will pause after a screenful of info. To continue with the next page, press [Spacebar]. To quit, type **q**.

There are additional things you can do with `more` at each break. The following table gives you a list of the commands you can give at the −More− (xx%) prompt and what they do.

Type	What It Does
Enter key	Displays only one more line rather than a whole screen.
a number followed by [Spacebar]	Displays that number of lines. For example, typing **5** and pressing [Spacebar] shows 5 more lines at the bottom of the screen.
h	Displays help.
/text	Search forward in the file for *text*. You must press [↵Enter] after this command.
n	Search for the next occurrence.
b	Skips back one screen.
=	Displays the current line number.
q	Quit.

You can use more as a *pipe* (with the pipe character ¦) to redirect output from another command to more. For example, if you have a large directory, you can type `ls -al ¦more` to see your directory listing a page at a time. Make sure that you do not put a space between the ¦ and more.

mv

Renames or moves files and directories.

mv: Moving a File to Different Directory

If you want to move a file to a different directory:

1. Type `mv`.

2. Press [Spacebar] and type the name of the file you want to move.

3. Press [Spacebar] and type the name of the directory where you want the file to be.

4. (Optional) Type a new file name in the other directory.

5. Press [↵Enter].

If you skip step 4, the file will have the same name as the original.

mv: Moving Multiple Files to Another Directory

You can move multiple files that have the same beginning part of the name with one command. For example, if you have 12 files named chap01.txt through chap12.txt, you can move them all at once. To do this, use wild cards, such as * and ?. The * stands for "zero or

more characters," while the ? stands for a single character. To do this:

1. Type mv.

2. Press [Spacebar] and type the wild-card specification of the files you want to move.

3. Press [Spacebar] and type the name of the
directory where you want the files to go.

4. Press [⏎Enter].

For example, to move 12 files named chap01.txt
through chap12.txt to the /backup directory, you
would type either mv **chap*.txt** /**backup** or mv
chap??.txt /**backup**.

mv: Renaming a File

If you've ftp'ed a file called lawyer.jokes.funniest
from an FTP site and you want to download it to your
PC, you need to rename it to a name that is acceptable
to DOS. The mv command can help.

To rename a file:

1. Type **mv**.

2. Press [Spacebar] and type the name of the file to
rename.

3. Press [Spacebar] and type the new name you
want the file to have.

4. Press [⏎Enter].

Typing mv **read.me readme.first** would rename
the file read.me to readme.first.

Very Important Safety Tip! Mv assumes you know
what you are doing. If you type **mv t.txt x.txt** and
x.txt already exists, mv will gladly overwrite it with
t.txt and not inform you. This is generally considered to be bad. To avoid this, use the -i switch (for
inquire) before you type the name of the file to
rename to cause mv to ask before overwriting. You
may think it should work this way by default, but it
doesn't.

passwd

Changes your password.

Passwords are an important aspect of computer security.
Change yours when you get a new account so that no
one can access your system.

Make sure your password is not easily guessed. Using
your name, or your spouse's is probably a bad idea.
You must, of course, make sure that you can remember it. The name of your favorite author isn't too bad.

To change your password:

1. Type **passwd**.

2. Press [↵Enter].

3. At the Old password: prompt, type your old
   password.

4. Press [↵Enter].

5. At the New password: prompt, type your new
   password and press [↵Enter].

6. When asked, type it again for verification and press
   [↵Enter].

Some systems have limits on passwords and it may reject your new password. Usually, these limits are there to ensure that a password is not too short, otherwise it could easily be cracked by someone trying all the combinations. If this happens, try another password until `passwd` accepts it.

pico

Edits a text file.

Are you familiar with Microsoft Word, Wordperfect or Ami Pro? Forget it. Editing text on UNIX is nothing like it. For one thing, the text editors don't allow you to format text—just type it and make changes to it. Second, no mice allowed. Everything is commands or arrow keys.

There are several editors under UNIX and pico is one of the easier and more popular ones. pico comes from Pine Composer, so you can correctly deduce that learning this editor will help you compose messages in the pine e-mail program.

Most of the commands in pico consist of control key combinations, such as Ctrl-x. To execute these, hold the control key (Ctrl) and press the other key at the same time. You don't need to hit ↵Enter.

To edit a file:

1. Type **pico**.

2. Press [Spacebar] and type the name of the file you want to edit.

3. Press ↵Enter.

If the file exists, pico will open it for you. If not, it creates a new file with that name. You will see a screen that looks like:

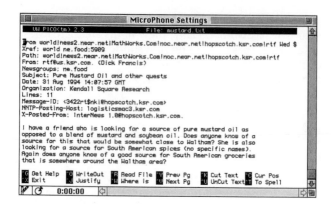

pico: Editing Text

When you type, the characters are automatically entered into the file. Pressing the [Del] key or [Ctrl]-[H] deletes the previous character. (It works like [←Backspace].) Pressing [Ctrl]-[D] deletes the current character to the right of the cursor. Pressing [Ctrl]-[K] cuts the entire line. [Ctrl]-[U] undeletes or pastes the last cut line.

To cut and paste text:

1. Press [Ctrl]-[^] (Also known as [Ctrl]-[⇧Shift]-[6]) to mark the beginning of a text block.

2. Move the cursor to the end of the block.

3. Press [Ctrl]-[K].

4. Move the cursor to where you want to paste the text.

5. Press [Ctrl]-[U].

If you use [Ctrl]-[K] to delete several lines in a row with no other actions in between, [Ctrl]-[U] uncuts (pastes) all the lines at once. You can use this as an alternate method of cutting and pasting. You must make sure you don't do any other cutting in between the [Ctrl]-[K] and [Ctrl]-[U].

pico: Importing Another Text File

To insert an existing text file into the middle of the file you are editing:

1. Position the cursor to where you want the file to be inserted.

2. Press Ctrl-R.

3. At the Insert File: prompt, type the file name to insert.

4. Press ↵Enter.

In case you forget the name of the file or where it is in your directory tree, at the Insert File: prompt, you can type Ctrl-T to bring you to a file list. This browser allows you to navigate around your directory structure to find a file.

pico: Moving Around Files

To move around the file, you use a number of different keys. The arrow keys work to move the cursor to a new position, or you can use the following commands:

Key to Type	Where It Moves the Cursor
Ctrl-B or →	Back one character
Ctrl-F or ←	Forward one character
Ctrl-P or ↑	To the previous line
Ctrl-N or ↓	To the next line
Ctrl-A	To the beginning of the current line
Ctrl-E	To the end of the current line

continues

Continued

Key to Type	Where It Moves the Cursor
Ctrl-Y	To the previous page of text
Ctrl-V	To the next page of text
Ctrl-Spacebar (the Space key)	To the next word

pico: Quitting pico

To exit pico:

1. Hit Ctrl-x.

2. If you see Save modified buffer (ANSWERING "No" WILL DESTROY CHANGES) (y/n)?, type **y** to save or **n** to cancel the changes.

3. If you typed **y** in step 2, press ↵Enter to accept the current name, or enter a new one and press ↵Enter.

pico: Saving Files

Editing a file wouldn't do much good if you didn't save it out.

To save a file in pico without quitting:

1. Press Ctrl-O.

2. At the File Name to write: prompt, type the name you want the file to have.

3. Press ↵Enter.

pico: Searching for Text in a File

To search for a string:

1. Press Ctrl-W.

2. At the Search: prompt, type the string to find.

3. Press ↵Enter.

Pico can only search forward, but it automatically wraps around to the beginning of the file when the search reaches the end of the file.

pine

Sending and receiving electronic mail.

pine is a much more robust program than UNIX mail for working with e-mail; use it if it is available. There are other mail programs, but pine is widely available on most Internet services. With pine, you can e-mail President Clinton on your ideas for health care reform or send an electronically scanned picture of your new baby to your friend in Boston (I've seen it done. Pretty cool).

To start pine:

1. Type **pine**.
2. Press ⏎Enter).

You will see the following screen:

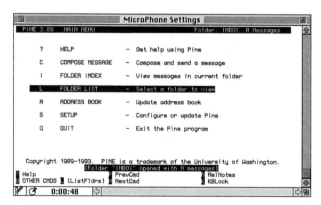

pine: Attaching Files to Messages

You may think that since pine comes with a nice little attachment line, that is how you should attach files. Wrong. Well, not really wrong, just limited. The problem is that unless your recipient is using pine or some other MIME (Multipurpose Internet Mail Extensions) enabled mail reader, they won't be able to receive your attachment. The following method for attaching files takes more steps but is universal.

> **BIG WARNING!!** Using this method, you can only send text (ASCII) files! You cannot send binary files without a special process (see uuencode). Use uuencode to convert a binary file to text. You then attach it using the method below and the recipient runs uudecode on the message to convert it back to binary (see uudecode).

To include a text file in a message:

1. Compose a message using steps 1–8 from *pine: Composing a Message*.

2. Instead of typing text, press `Ctrl`-`R`.

3. At the `Insert file:` prompt, type the name of the file you want to include.

4. Press `⏎Enter`.

5. When your message is complete, press `Ctrl`-`X`.

6. At the `Send message? [y]:` prompt, type **y** or press `⏎Enter` to send the message. Press `n` if you want to abort sending.

A copy of the mail you sent is automatically stored in the `sent-mail` folder.

In case you forget the name of the file or where it is in your directory tree, at the `Insert File:` prompt, you can type `Ctrl`-`T` to bring you to a file browser. This browser allows you to navigate around your directory structure to find a file.

pine: Composing a Message

"Tis better to give than to receive," or so they say. Sending a message using pine is simple. You must know the address of the person to whom you are sending, though (see e-mail addresses in "The Least You Need to Know," at the front of this book).

To send a message:

1. At the main menu, the Folder index, or within a message, type **c**.

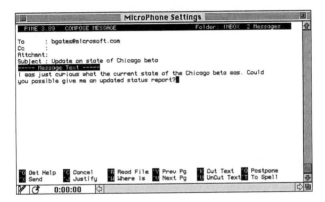

2. On the To: line, type the recipient's e-mail address.

3. (Optional) For multiple recipients, press comma (⎽,⎽) and type an additional address.

4. Press the ⏎Enter to move to the Cc: line.

5. (Optional) Type the carbon copy recipients' e-mail addresses, separated by commas.

6. Press ⏎Enter twice to move beyond the Attchmnt: line to Subject:.

Why step 6? See *pine: Attaching Files to Messages* for the reason.

7. At the Subject: prompt, type the subject of your message.

8. Press ⏎Enter.

9. Type in the text of your message.

Tip

In step 9, here you are in the pico editor. See *pico* for more details about using this editor.

10. When your message is complete, press Ctrl-X.
11. At the `Send message? [y]:` prompt, type **y** or press ↵Enter to send the message, or **n** to abort sending.

A copy of the mail you sent is automatically stored in the *sent-mail* folder.

Tip

If you want to cancel the sending of a message before you finish, press Ctrl-C.

pine: Creating an Address Book

pine has a nice feature that lets you create an address book so you don't have to remember all the obscure e-mail addresses of your friends and relatives.

To get to the address book, type **A** from the main menu. You will see a screen that looks like:

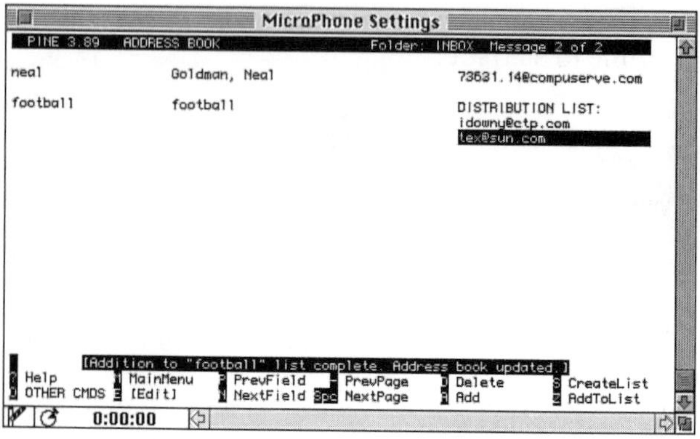

To add a person's address to your address book:

1. Type **A**.

2. At the `New full name (last, first):` prompt, type the name of the person who you want in the address book. Type in the last name and first name separated by a comma.

3. Press [⏎Enter].

4. At the `Enter new nickname:` prompt, type a one word nickname for this person.

5. Press [⏎Enter].

To create a distribution list of multiple people:

1. Type **S**.

2. At the `Enter Descriptive Name:` prompt, type in a name for your mailing list.

3. At the `Enter new nickname:` prompt, type a one word nickname for this mailing list.

4. At the `Enter address:` prompt, type in the first address of your mailing list.

5. Press [⏎Enter].

6. (Optional) Continue adding addresses, followed by [⏎Enter].

7. Press [⏎Enter] to finish.

To add an address to a mailing list:

1. Select the mailing list using the cursor keys.

2. Type **Z**.

3. At the `Address to add to 'x' list:` prompt, type the new e-mail address to add.

4. Press [⏎Enter].

To use an address from the mailing list in a message:

1. In the `To:` field as you are composing a message, type in the nickname of the address you want to use instead of the full address.

2. Press (↵Enter).

Pine will automatically substitute the full address for the nickname you specified.

pine: Deleting Messages

It's imperative that you periodically delete old e-mail messages, otherwise they clog up your system and take up extra disk space.

To delete a message:

1. If you are in the Mail Index, select the message which you want to delete. If you are already viewing the message, fine.

2. Type **D**. A D will appear next to the message.

If you accidentally delete a message, just undelete it. Type **u** instead of **d** in step 2. The D next to the message will disappear. Also, when you quit pine, the program asks you again whether you actually want to delete the messages that you requested be deleted. You can say no at that point as well.

pine: Forwarding a Message

To forward a message:

1. If you are in the Folder Index, select the message to which you want to forward. If you are already viewing the message, fine.

2. Type **F**.

3. Type the forwardee's e-mail address.

4. (Optional) For multiple recipients, press comma (,) and type an additional address.

5. (Optional) In the Message Text area, you can add some additional text to precede the forwarded message.

6. Press (Ctrl)-(X).

7. At the Send message? [y]: prompt, type **y** or press (↵Enter) to send the message or type **n** to abort sending.

pine: Managing Folders

Pine keeps several folders around and moves messages automatically between them. The folder that contains new e-mail is called INBOX. There are three other folders:

➤ saved-messages is the default folder if you want to store an INBOX message in a folder.

➤ read-messages is automatically updated with messages that you have read.

➤ sent-messages is automatically updated with a copy of any message you send.

It's up to you to manage these folders and not let too much old mail collect in them.

To save a message in a folder:

1. If you are in the Mail Index, select the message which you want to export. If you are already viewing the message, fine.

2. Type **S**.

3. At the SAVE to folder [saved-messages] : prompt, type the folder you want to save the message into.

4. Press ⏎Enter.

Skip step 3 above if you want the message to go into the saved-messages folder.

To move to a particular folder:

1. At the Folder Index, or while viewing a message, type **L**.

2. Press the ⬆ or ⬇ key to select a folder.

3. Press ⏎Enter.

You will see a list of messages for that folder. Work with them exactly as you do for the messages in INBOX.

pine: Quitting Pine

Since pine doesn't permanently make any changes in deleting or moving messages until you quit, when you quit, you are asked a bunch of questions about the changes you made in order to confirm your actions.

To quit pine:

1. Type **q**.

2. Type **y**.

3. (Optional) Type **y** at the Save the 'x' read message (s) in "read-messages" prompt to copy read messages to the read-messages folder.

4. (Optional) At the Expunge the 'x' deleted message (s) from INBOX? prompt, type **y** to delete the messages marked for deletion.

If you have deleted messages in other folders, you will have to answer "expunge" questions for each folder.

pine: Reading E-Mail Messages

When you start pine, it automatically opens a folder called inbox. This is where all your incoming messages reside.

To read your e-mail messages:

1. At the main menu, type **i** for the Folder Index screen.

2. Press ⬆ or ⬇ to highlight the message you want.

3. Press ⏎Enter to view the highlighted message.

You can press n for "next message" or p for "previous message" as an alternative to the up and down arrow keys.

If you are so popular that your message list goes beyond one screen, hit ⬚Spacebar⬚ to move to the next screen of messages and a hyphen (⬚-⬚) to move to the previous screen. To jump to a particular message, type **j**. Pine will prompt you for the message number. Type it and press ⏎Enter.

pine: Replying to a Message

If you decide that you need to reply to the urgent e-mail request for your presence at the White House, you can easily do so within pine.

In general, netiquette says that you should include the previous message, or at least a portion of it, in the reply so the recipient can remember what you are replying to.

To reply to a message:

1. If you are in the Folder Index, select the message to which you want to reply. If you are already viewing the message, fine.

2. Press R. Pine responds with: Include original message in Reply? (y/n/^C) [n]:

3. Type **y** if you want to include the original message, **n** if you don't.

In step 3, if you just press ⏎Enter, pine will not
include the original. If you choose {yes}, pine will
insert a > in front of each line of the previous message
to differentiate it.

4. Type the text of your reply.

5. When your reply is complete, press Ctrl-X.

6. At the Send message? [y]: prompt, type y or press
   ⏎Enter to send the message. Type n if you want to
   abort sending.

pine: Saving a Message to a File

Pine lets you store messages in a variety of folders (see
pine: Managing Folders), but sometimes you want to save
a message out as a file. For example, if someone e-mailed
you an uuencoded binary file, you need to store it out as
a text file and run uudecode on it.

To save a message to a text file:

1. If you are in the FolderIndex, select the message
   which you want to export. If you are already
   viewing the message, fine.

2. Type **E**.

3. At the File (in home directory) to save
   message text in: prompt, type the name of the
   file you want to save the message as.

4. Press ⏎Enter.

pine: Signature Files

Many people like to attach a unique signature to every
mail message they send. Usually these include your full
name, address, and some witty quote.

If you have a text file called `.signature` in your home directory, pine will automatically include it at the end of every message you send. A typical signature file may look like:

— —

```
jlupner@netcom.com ¦"The trouble with the rat
race is that

Jan Lupner         ¦ even if you win, you're
still a rat.

(617) 566-8492     ¦            .....Lily Tomlin
```

— —

To create a signature file, use pico or vi to edit the signature file (see pico or vi). You should make sure the file is reasonably short because it will be included in every message. Also, you should keep the length of each line under 60 characters to ensure that it looks good on everyone's screen.

pwd

Displays the current working directory

If you've navigated your way through many levels of directory and find yourself lost, the `pwd` command tells you what your current directory is.

To print the working directory:

1. At the UNIX prompt, type **pwd**.
2. Press ⏎Enter.

rm

Deletes files from a directory

It's definitely easier to destroy than to create. In UNIX, there are no Norton Utilities or undelete mechanisms to recover files if you accidentally delete them. Be careful.

To delete a file:

1. Type **rm**.

2. (Optional) Press and type **-i**.

>
>
> The **-i** switch will prompt you for a confirmation on any files you delete. It can be a pain if you have a lot of files, but losing an essential file is more painful.

3. Press ⟨ Spacebar ⟩ and type the name of the file to delete.

4. Press ⟨↵Enter⟩.

> **Try This!**
>
> If you have 12 files named `chap01.txt` through `chap12.txt`, you can delete them all at once. To do this, use wild cards, such as * and ?. The * stands for zero or more characters, while the ? stands for a single character. To delete the 12 files, type either **rm chap*.txt** or **rm chap??.txt** and press ⟨↵Enter⟩.

rmdir

Removes a directory.

To delete a directory:

1. Delete all the files in the directory using the **rm** comand.

2. Type **rmdir**.

3. Press ⟨ Spacebar ⟩ and type the name of the directory you want to delete.

4. Press ⟨↵Enter⟩.

THIS TIP IS EXCEEDINGLY DANGEROUS! USE WITH
CAUTION!!!! If you want to delete all the files in a
directory and all the files and subdirectories in it with
one terribly destructive command, you can type
rm -r -i followed by the name of the directory and
press ⏎Enter. This will delete everything in the
directory and subdirectories in one fell swoop. If you
leave off the **-i**, you won't even be prompted for a
confirmation. **I REPEAT. USE THIS ONLY IF YOU**
REALLY **KNOW WHAT YOU'RE DOING!**

rn

Reads USENET Newsgroups

Before you read any further, see if you have access to the
tin newsreader (type **tin** and press ⏎Enter at your UNIX
prompt). If you do, skip this section and go to tin. It's
much easier and better to use than rn.

I included rn to ensure that those unfortunate enough
not to have access to tin are covered somewhat. Not to
say that tin is the ultimate newsreader. It's not, but it's
much better than rn (in my humble opinion).

rn: Marking Articles

Reading an article marks it as read. You will not see it in
the list of messages next time you read the newsgroup.
You can also mark articles as read so that you don't have
to ever read them.

➤ To mark a given article and all its replies as read,
type a comma (**,**).

➤ To mark all the remaining articles in the
newsgroup as read, type **c** (for catchup).

➤ To mark all articles with the same title as read,
type **k**.

rn: Posting an Article on a Different Subject

What if you want to start your own discussion in a newsgroup on a different topic? Well, you can. Just make sure that the topic falls in the domain of the newsgroup to which you are posting. If you don't, the readers of the newsgroup will send you nasty notes.

To post a new article:

1. Navigate to a newsgroup and read an article there.

2. Type **f** (make sure it's lowercase). Technically, rn thinks you're replying, but it gives you the option of starting a new subject.

3. At the `Are you starting an unrelated topic?` question, type **y**.

4. Press (⏎Enter).

5. At the `Subject:` prompt, type the subject of your new topic.

6. Press (⏎Enter).

7. At the `Distribution:` prompt, press (⏎Enter).

8. (Optional) If asked if you are sure, type **y**. This message may not appear.

9. Press (⏎Enter).

10. At the `Prepared file to include [none]:` prompt, press (⏎Enter).

11. Create your message in the editor program that appears.

12. Close your editor.

13. At the `Send, abort, edit or list?` prompt, type **s** to send the posting.

> See *rn: Selecting a Text Editor* to learn how to choose
> which editor appears in step 11.

An alternate method of posting an article is to use the
pnews command from the UNIX prompt. The only
differences between using the f command in rn and
pnews is that the first question that pnews asks you is the
name of the newsgroup to which you want to post and
that it gives you a list of possible distributions.

rn: Reading Articles

To read an article in a newsgroup, you must be at a
prompt that looks like:

```
****** 9100 unread articles in ne.forsale — read
now? [ynq]
```

To read the first unread article:

1. Type **y** or press <u>Spacebar</u>. If you type **n**, you
   will be prompted to read the next newsgroup.

To navigate from the article, you can type one of the
following commands:

Command	Where It Takes You
Space	If you are not at the end of the article, you will see the next page of the article. If you are at the end of the article, you will go to the next unread article.
b	Back up one page.
n	The next unread article.
N	The next article.
Ctrl-N	The next unread article with the same subject heading.

continues

Continued

Command	Where It Takes You
P	The previous article.
Ctrl-P	The previous article with the same subject.
$	The end of the newsgroup.
^	The first unread message.
q	Leaves this article or newsgroup.
=	Shows a list of the messages by number in the newsgroup.
(Number)	Typing the number of an article and pressing ⏎Enter takes you to that article.

rn: Replying to an Article

The great part about newsgroups is that anyone can throw their two cents in. To make your mark on the world and have your words read by thousands of people, all you need to do is reply to a message.

To reply to an article:

1. Type **F** (make sure it's uppercase) to include a copy of the original message as part of your reply.

2. If you see a warning message that asks if you really want to reply, type **y**.

3. At the Prepared file to include [none]: prompt, press ⏎Enter.

In step 3, if you really *have* prepared a file in advance, type the name of the file and press ⏎Enter. That would be more foresight than most of us have.

4. Type your response in the editor program that appears.

5. Close the editor. (See the section in this book for your particular editor.)

6. At the `Send, abort, edit or list?` prompt, type **s** to send the posting.

rn: Saving an Article to a File

If you are in the middle of an exciting article and decide to save it to a file:

1. Type **s**.

2. Press ⌐ Spacebar ⌐ and type the name file to which you want to save the message.

3. Press ⌐Enter⌐.

4. Type **y** at the `Use mailbox format?` question.

rn will save the file in the News directory under your home directory.

rn: Searching for an Article

You can search for an article with a particular subject or a newsgroup with a particular name. The command is the same. If you are at the newsgroup level, you will search for group names. If you are at the article level, you will search for subjects. To search:

1. Type **/**.

2. Type the string you are looking for.

3. Press ⌐Enter⌐.

Try This!

Typing **/ne.food** at an unread articles in
newsgroup— read now? prompt would look for the
newsgroup ne.food so you can read the articles in it.
Doing the same thing while you were reading an
article would look for another article in the
newsgroup that had the string ne.food in the
subject.

rn: Selecting a Text Editor

The text editor that rn uses is defined by the EDITOR
environment variable in UNIX. To set this from the
UNIX % prompt:

1. Type **setenv EDITOR**.

2. Press [Spacebar] and type the name of your
   favorite editor, be it pico, vi or something else.

3. Press [⏎Enter].

rn: Some News Group Basics

To read any of these newsgroups, you must subscribe to
them. The list of newsgroups is everchanging and every
time you start rn, you will be asked if you want to
subscribe to any of the newsgroups that have appeared
since the last time you ran rn.

The list of newsgroups you subscribe to is in a file called
.newsrc. Some service providers create this list for you
by default, or when you first run rn, it will be created for
you. You can look at or edit the file (see cat, more, pico
or vi). Your .newsrc file may look like:

```
news.announce.newusers! 1-997
ne.food! 1-5653
ne.forsale! 1-18509
ne.general! 1-9134
ne.housing: 1-5347
ne.jobs: 1-6066
ne.news: 1-457
ne.org.decus: 1-75
```

You are subscribed to any newsgroup that has a : after it and not subscribed to any with a !.

rn: Starting and Subscribing to Newsgroups

To start rn:

1. Type **rn**.

2. Press [⏎Enter].

3. (Optional) If there are new newsgroups available, rn asks you whether you want to subscribe each one. At each one, you have the option of typing one of the following:

   y to subscribe to the newsgroup

   Y to subscribe to all the newsgroups

   n to not subscribe to this newsgroup

   N to subscribe to none of the newsgroups.

You will then see a screen that looks like:

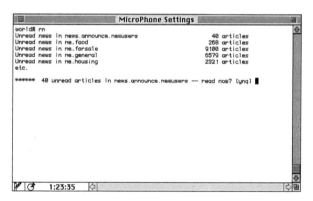

To subscribe to a new newsgroup:

1. At any `x unread articles in newsgroup— read now? [ynq]` prompt, type **g**.

2. Press [Spacebar] and type the name of the newsgroup you want to subscribe to.

3. Press [⏎Enter].

![Try This!]

You can use wild cards in subscribing to newsgroups. For example, typing **g ne.*** would subscribe to any newsgroups that had the string "ne." followed by any number of characters.

To unsubscribe to a newsgroup:

1. At any x unread articles in newsgroup— read now? [ynq] prompt, type **u**.

rx

Uploads a file from your computer to your service provider's using XMODEM.

If you dial in to a service provider and your communications software supports ZMODEM, stop here and go read about rz.

You have this great file on your PC that you'd love to mail to someone. How do you get it up to your service provider's computer? Rx is the cure. It will upload the file to your service provider using the XMODEM protocol.

To upload a file:

1. Type **rx**.

2. (Optional) Press ⟨ Spacebar ⟩ and type **-a** if you are transferring an ASCII text file.

3. Press ⟨ Spacebar ⟩ and type the name to give the file on the service provider's disk.

4. Press ⟨ ↵Enter ⟩.

5. Start sending the file using your communications software.

What you actually do in step 5 will depend on which software you are using, but there is usually a Transfer

menu item for the software. Make sure that the protocol
is set for XMODEM and that if you have specified **-a**,
that you send the file as text.

rz

*Uploading a file from your computer to your service provider's
using ZMODEM.*

If you have a file on your PC, you need to transfer it to
your service provider's computer before you can e-mail it
to anyone. rz is the cure. It will upload the file to your
service provider using the ZMODEM protocol.

ZMODEM is better than XMODEM in several ways:

➤ It's faster.

➤ You don't need to specify the name of the file to
receive.

➤ You can send multiple files at a time.

To upload a file:

1. Type **rz**.

2. (Optional) Press ⌷ Spacebar ⌷ and type **-a** if you
are transferring an ASCII text file.

3. Press ⌷⏎Enter⌷.

4. Start sending the files using your communications
software.

The actual procedure to use in step 4 depends on which
software you are using, but there is usually a Transfer
menu item for the software. Make sure that the protocol
is set for ZMODEM and that if you have specified **-a**,
that you send the file as text.

rz automatically uses the names that the files have on
your PC. Beware that the file names may contain characters that aren't allowed on the receiving computer.

split

Splits files into smaller chunks for transmission.

Some e-mail systems have limits on the size of messages
that you can send to or from them. This can be a
problem when you are sending files. To fix this, you
must split your file into pieces, send the pieces, and then
have the recipient reassemble the file using the `cat`
command. For some reason, though, if you name a file
humpty-dumpty, this doesn't work.

To split a file into pieces:

1. Type **split**.

2. (Optional) Press ⌴Spacebar⌴ and type a dash (-)
   followed by the number of lines you want in each
   file.

> In step 2, you must make sure you don't add a space
> between the dash and the number. The default
> number of lines is 1000, which is what `split` will use
> if you skip step 2.

3. Press ⌴Spacebar⌴ and type the name of the file
   you want to split.

4. (Optional) Press ⌴Spacebar⌴ and type the root
   name of the output files. `Split` will automatically
   add letters to the end of the file name.

5. Press ⌴Enter⌴.

`Split` will split the input file into as many files as
necessary, appending the letters aa, ab, ac, and so on to
the end of each file. If you ignore the output file option,
`split` assigns the letter x to be the first part of the
output file names, generating files called xaa, xab, and so
on.

For example, **split -500 toobig.txt rightsize**
would split the file `toobig.txt` into 500-line chunks
and create a series of files called `rightsizeaa`,
`rightsizeab`, `rightsizeac`, and so on.

swais

Searches a Wide Area Information Server (WAIS) for databases.

As you've no doubt seen, finding things on the Internet
is not easy. So users came up with a mechanism where
you could search databases over the Internet by keyword. The big gotcha is finding the right keywords.

swais: Searching Databases

To search for keywords, you must first select the databases in which you want to search.

To initiate a search:

1. Navigate through the list of databases until you
    find a database that has a name that looks appro-
    priate for the area in which your desired topic is
    located. Use the following keys to move around
    the list:

What to Type	Where the Cursor Goes
j or ⬇	Down one entry
J	Down one screen
k	Up one entry
K	Up one screen
number	Move to the entry of that number
/	Searches for string in the database name
v	View information about the database

2. Press [Spacebar] to select the entry as a database for searching. An asterisk (*) will appear next to the entry.

3. (Optional) Repeat steps 1 and 2 until all the databases you want to search are selected.

4. Type **w** and press (⏎Enter).

5. Type the keywords for which you want to search.

6. Press (⏎Enter).

You can specify multiple keywords, including Boolean expressions; so you can search for the recipes database for "ketchup apples" or "ketchup and apples." The first will find recipes that have either ketchup or apples; the second would only find those with both. Yuck.

swais: To Start a WAIS Search

1. Type **swais**.

2. Press (⏎Enter).

You will see a screen that looks like this:

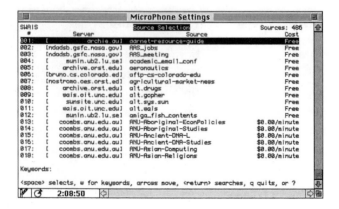

> If your service provider doesn't provide swais, you
> can telnet to a server that does. Type **telnet
> quake.think.com** and press ⏎Enter. At the login:
> prompt, type **wais**.

swais: Viewing the Results of a Search

If the WAIS search is successful, swais returns with a list
of documents in the databases. Each document has a
score associated with it that indicates how many
matches it seems to have against your keyword. The
higher the score, the better (this isn't golf).

To retrieve a document from the database:

1. Navigate to the document in the list.

2. Press ⏎Enter.

3. Type **q** to return to the document list.

sx

*Downloads a file from your service provider to your computer
using XMODEM.*

If you dial in to a service provider and your communications software supports ZMODEM, stop reading here and
go read about sz.

You downloaded this great file using ftp and you can't
get it to your PC? Sx will save you. It will download the
file from your service provider using the XMODEM
protocol.

To download a file:

1. Type **sx**.

2. (Optional) Press ⌷ Spacebar ⌷ and type **-a** if you
   are transferring an ASCII text file.

3. Press [Spacebar] and type the name of the file you want to send.

4. Press [↵Enter].

5. Start receiving the file using your communications software.

Step 5 will differ depending on which software you are using, but there is usually a Transfer menu item for the software. Make sure that the protocol is set for XMODEM and that if you have specified -a, that you receive the file as text.

sz

Downloads a file from your service provider to your computer using ZMODEM.

You downloaded this great file using ftp and you can't get it to your PC? sz will save you. It will download the file from your service provider using the ZMODEM protocol.

ZMODEM is better than XMODEM in several ways:

➤ It's faster.

➤ You don't need to specify the name of the file to receive.

➤ You can send multiple files at a time.

To download a file:

1. Type **sz**.

2. (Optional) Press [Spacebar] and type **-a** if you are transferring an ASCII text file.

3. Press [Spacebar] and type the name of the file you want to send.

4. Press [↵Enter].

5. Start receiving the files using your communications software.

Step 5 will differ depending on which software you are using, but there is usually a Transfer menu item for the software. Make sure that the protocol is set for ZMODEM and that if you have specified ·a, that you receive the file as text. Often with ZMODEM, the transfer will start automatically without you specifically receiving the file.

Sz will automatically use the names that the files have on your service provider. Beware that the file names may contain characters that aren't allowed on your PC.

> With ZMODEM, you can send multiple files at once. To do this, add the names after the first one on the command line. Or you can use wild cards like *.txt. Typing **sz -a a.txt b.txt** would send both files to your PC.

telnet

Logs into other computers and use their resources.

What happens if the computer you are connected to on the Internet doesn't have the utility you want, such as ARCHIE? You can call up the system administrator for your Internet provider and complain, but that probably won't help you much. An easier way is to telnet to another computer that does have ARCHIE and use it, exactly as if you were sitting at that computer.

When you use telnet, your computer becomes a *client* and the other computer becomes a *server*. Anything that you type on your keyboard (client) is directly sent to the server for processing. Anything the server writes back is immediately sent to the client and appears on your screen. All your computer is doing is acting as a bridge between your keyboard and the host.

telnet: Changing Line-by-Line or Character-at-a-Time Mode

Most of the time, telnet wants to send information to the host a character at a time, and it starts up this way. Some older computers only want to receive it a line at time. To switch to line-by-line mode:

1. At the telnet> prompt, type **mode line**.

2. Press ⏎Enter.

To reverse, just type **mode character** in step 1.

telnet: Changing Local Echo

Normally, when you type a character, the client picks it up, sends it to the host, who acknowledges receipt and sends it back to your screen for display. This is called *remote echoing*. If both sides don't agree on remote echoing, you may see two characters (both local and remote are displaying) or no characters (both assume the other will display and don't).

To change echoing:

1. Press ⌘-⌑ (or whatever your current escape sequence is).

2. Type **set echo**.

3. Press ⏎Enter.

4. Press ⏎Enter again to return to the host.

To set telnet back again, repeat the process.

telnet: Changing the Escape Sequence

Perhaps you have something against ⌘-⌑? Perhaps the escape sequence contains keys necessary for work on your new host. Whatever. You want to change the sequence.

To change the escape sequence:

1. At the `telnet>` prompt, type **set escape**.

2. Press [Spacebar] and type the character you want as the new escape sequence

3. Press [⏎Enter].

For control characters, you can type ^**x** (the caret followed by an x) or you can actually hit the sequence ⌘-[x].

telnet: Logging Out from the Host

When you finish with telnet, you need to logout from the host and close the connection. Simple, right? Sort of. In the grand world of the Internet, nothing is simple, so we're going to give you several options to choose from. Since you don't know how the telnet site is going to work, you don't necessarily know how to logout in advance. One of these should work.

To logout from the host:

1. Type one of the following: **logout**, **bye**, **quit**, **exit**, **g**, **goodbye**, **logoff**, **done**, **stop**, or **disconnect**.

2. Press [⏎Enter].

One of these should close your connection and return you to your machine.

If you are stuck on the host computer and nothing seems to work to close the connection, try the following:

1. Press ⌘-[]] (or whatever your current escape sequence is).

2. Type **close** or **quit**.

3. Press [⏎Enter].

The escape sequence brings you back to the `telnet>` prompt on your computer.

telnet: Make a Remote Connection

To telnet to a remote computer:

1. Type **telnet**.

2. Press the ⌷ Spacebar ⌷ and type the host computer address.

3. (Optional) Press ⌷ Spacebar ⌷ and type the port number.

4. Press ⌷↵Enter⌷.

For the host address, you can use either the normal domain address (such as **wylbur.cu.nih.gov**) or the numeric IP address (such as **128.231.64.82**), if you have it. Either works, but the domain address is almost certainly easier to remember unless you're an accountant.

Sometimes, a telnet site will have multiple ports on the host computer to keep services separate. If there is more than one port, you need to specify the one you want.

For example, to connect to the Cornell CWIS, you would type, **telnet cuinfo.cornell.edu 300**. The only way to know if you need another port is if you are told when you find out about the telnet site.

If you are at the telnet> prompt, you can connect to another host by typing **open** in step 1 instead of exiting and starting over. Make sure you "close" any other telnet connection first.

When you telnet, you should see something such as this (your text and mileage may vary, plus tax, void where prohibited):

```
                        MicroPhone Settings
world% telnet culine.colorado.edu 859
Trying 128.138.129.170...
Connected to CUBoulder.colorado.edu.
Escape character is '^]'.

Teams can specified with or without leading -t, from the following list:
atl-Atlanta Hawks        bos-Boston Celtics       cha-Charlotte Hornets
chi-Chicago Bulls        cle-Cleveland Cavaliers  dal-Dallas Mavericks
den-Denver Nuggets       det-Detroit Pistons      g.s-GoldenState Warriors
hou-Houston Rockets      ind-Indiana Pacers       lac-L.A. Clippers
lal-L.A. Lakers          mia-Miami Heat           mil-Milwaukee Bucks
min-Minn. Timberwolves   nj -New Jersey Nets      ny -New York Knicks
orl-Orlando Magic        phi-Phil. 76ers          pho-Phoenix Suns
por-Portland Trailblazers sac-Sacramento Kings    san-SanAntonio Spurs
sea-Seattle Supersonics  uta-Utah Jazz            was-Washington Bullets
Divisions can specified with or without a leading -d, from the following list:
       pac - Pacific        mdw - Mid West
       ctl - Central        atc - Atlantic

Welcome to the National Basketball Association Schedule Service.
<nba>
```
` 0:00:00 `

You may be asked for a terminal type (no it's not asking about a fatal illness). Generally, you should choose VT100, which is the most common terminal type. Macintosh users should choose VT102.

telnet: Stopping Something You Started on the Host

Sometimes, you start something on the host and don't realize what the results might be. If you start something you don't want to finish, you can interrupt the host by issuing the appropriate *break* sequence. There is, of course, no standard break sequence across computers. That would be too easy.

For most Unix computers, to break the program:

1. Press ⌘-C.

Be careful not to type too many too quickly. This can sometimes cause your telnet connection to be broken.

If that doesn't work, try the following:

1. Press ⌘-☐ (or whatever your current escape sequence is).

2. Type **send brk**.

3. Press ⏎Enter.

This requests that telnet send a break sequence to the host. Depending on the state of the host, this may or may not work.

telnet: Suspending Telnet Temporarily

When you are working in telnet, you may want to go back to your original system and do something there. Perhaps you've asked the host computer to do something that will take a long time and you don't want to sit around and wait.

To temporarily suspend the connection between your keyboard and the host computer, you need to hit the *escape* key sequence.

This is different on each computer, but for most Unix systems, to escape:

1. Press ⌘-☐.

2. Press ⏎Enter.

This should bring you back to a `telnet>` prompt on your computer.

To temporarily suspend telnet on your computer so that you can do something at the operating system level:

1. At the `telnet>` prompt, type **z**.

2. Press ⏎Enter.

Through all this, the telnet connection is still maintained in the background while you do your local work.

To return to the `telnet>` prompt, from the operating
system:

1. type **fg**.
2. Press ⏎Enter.

To return to your host from the `telnet>` prompt:

1. Press ⏎Enter.

> The host will usually print out what the escape
> sequence is as you login. Watch for it and write it
> down if it is different. For example,
>
> ```
> % telnet access.usask.ca
> Trying 128.233.3.1...
> Connected to access.usask.ca
> Escape character is '^]'.
> ```

telnet: VM/XA SP ONLINE...

Some telnet hosts are IBM mainframes running what is
know as 3270 software. If you see the line `VM/XA SP
ONLINE ...`, the machine you've hooked to is an IBM
mainframe.

You will need to run a special version of telnet, called
`tn3270`. With `tn3270`, you work similarly, but you may
need to work with your service provider to help with the
arcane IBM speak.

tin

Reads USENET Newsgroups.

To read any newsgroups, you need a newsreader. There
are lots of them out there, but tin is one of the better
ones.

tin: Managing Your Subscription List

With close to 10,000 newsgroups available, managing the list of groups you subscribe to is essential. Imagine if you subscribed to every magazine in the Publisher's Clearinghouse. Ed McMahon would be happy, but you'd drown in paper.

To unsubscribe from a newsgroup:

1. At the newsgroup list, navigate to the newsgroup to which you want to unsubscribe (see navigation).

2. Type **u**. A u will appear next to the newsgroup name.

If you have many newsgroups to unsubscribe:

1. At the newsgroup list, type **U**.

2. At the Enter regex unsubscribe pattern> prompt, type the name of the newsgroups to which you want to unsubscribe.

3. Press ⏎Enter.

You can enter a regular expression (see regular expressions in ARCHIE) including wild cards as part of the pattern. For example, to unsubscribe to all newsgroups that begin with alt., enter **alt.***.

To subscribe to a newsgroup:

1. At the newsgroup list, type **S**.

2. At the Enter regex subscribe pattern> prompt, type the name of the newsgroups to which you want to subscribe.

3. Press ⏎Enter.

You can enter a regular expression (see regular expressions in ARCHIE) including wild cards as part of the pattern. For example, to subscribe to all newsgroups that begin with `alt.`, enter **alt.***.

To subscribe to a newsgroup when you don't know its name:

1. At the newsgroup list, type **y**.

2. On the list that appears, select the one to which you want to subscribe.

3. Press **s**.

The list of newsgroups you subscribe to is in a file called `.newsrc`. When you first run tin, it will be created for you. You can look at or edit the file (see *cat*, *more*, *pico* or *vi*). Your `.newsrc` file may look like:

```
news.announce.newusers! 1-997

ne.food! 1-5653

ne.forsale! 1-18509

ne.general! 1-9134

ne.housing: 1-5347

ne.jobs: 1-6066

ne.news: 1-457

ne.org.decus: 1-75
```

You are subscribed to any newsgroup that has a : after it and not subscribed to any with a !.

tin: Marking Messages as Read

Once you have read an article, it will not show up in your list anymore. However, if you don't read all the articles, they will continue to haunt you. With a few well-chosen keystrokes, you can remove these blight articles from sight.

To mark an article as read, type **K**.

To mark an article as unread, type **z**.

To mark all articles as read, type **c** (for catchup).

tin: Reading Articles

To read an article in a newsgroup, you must navigate through the list of newsgroups and then through a list of articles in the newsgroup. Articles are organized as lists of related subject listings called *threads*. Threads make it easy to follow a discussion on a particular topic.

The navigation commands at each of the levels in tin are much the same. They are:

Command	Navigation
Spacebar , ⌘-D	Move down one page. If you are at the end of an article, Spacebar will move you to the next article.
b, ⌘-U	Move up one page.
k, ↑	Move up one line.
j, ↓	Move down one line.
x	Moves to newsgroup or thread number x. You must press ↵Enter after this command.
$	To the end of the list.
g newsgroup	Prompts for the name of the newsgroup to go to. Type the name of the newsgroup and press ↵Enter. Only works at the newsgroup list level.
/	Searches for text. Prompts for the string to look for. Type the text you want to find and press ↵Enter.

Command	Navigation
q	Quit the level. If you are reading an article, q takes you to the thread list. If you are at the newgroup level, q quits tin.
n	Move to the next article (only works while reading an article).
N	Move to the next unread article (only works while reading an article).
p	Move to the previous article (only works while reading an article).

To read an article:

1. Select the newsgroup that contains articles you want to read.

2. Press ⏎Enter.

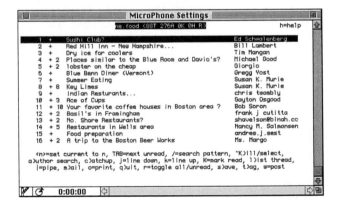

3. Select the thread that contains articles that have a subject you want to explore.

4. Press ⏎Enter.

5. (Optional) To move to the next article, type **n**, **N**, or press ⎵Spacebar⎵ if you are at the end of the article.

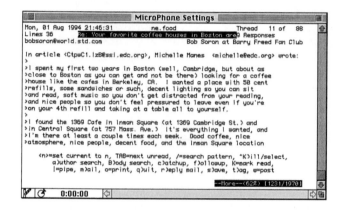

If you want to see the list of articles in a thread, type **1.** when you have selected it. You can then navigate through the list and only read some articles. This can prevent you from rereading the complete thread when someone posts a new response to a thread.

tin: Posting a New Article

If you want to start your own discussion in a newsgroup, post a new message. Make sure that your message will be perceived as appropriate by the members of the newsgroup. Otherwise, you will soon understand what it means to be flamed.

To start your own discussion thread:

1. At the thread list or in an article, type **w**.

2. At the Post subject []> prompt, type in a subject heading.

3. Press ⏎Enter.

4. You will be sent to your editor with a template for a message. Edit the text of your message.

5. Exit the editor.

6. At the q)uit, e)dit, p)ost: prompt, type **p**.

tin: Posting a Response

To throw your opinion into the fray, pick an article to which you absolutely feel compelled to respond and reply.

To post a response to an article:

1. Type **f**.

2. In the editor that appears, type your response.

Tin will already have copied the original message into your response. If it is too long, you should cut it down to avoid making your response too large.

3. Exit your editor.

4. At the q)uit, e)dit, p)ost: prompt, type **p**.

To respond by e-mail directly to the person who posted the message, rather than back to the newsgroup, type **r** in step 1 instead of **f**.

tin: Saving Articles to Files

To save an article to a file:

1. Type **s**.

2. At the `Save Filename[]>` prompt, type the name you want the article saved as.

3. Press ⏎Enter. You will see a prompt that looks like:

   ```
   Save a)rticle, t)hread, h)ot, p)attern,
   T)agged articles, q)uit: a
   ```

4. Type **a** or press ⏎Enter. Tin then prompts you with:

   ```
   Process n)one, s)har, u)ud, l)ist zoo, e)xt
   zoo, L)ist zip, E)xt zip, q)uit: n
   ```

5. Type **n** or press ⏎Enter.

   Tin will save the file in your News directory.

If you want to save multiple articles, type **t** at each article to tag it. Then, type **T** in step 4, rather than **a**.

tin: Selecting an Editor

The text editor that `tin` uses is defined by the EDITOR environment variable in Unix. To set this:

1. At the UNIX prompt, type **setenv EDITOR**.

2. Press ⸤ Spacebar ⸥ and type the name of your favorite editor, be it pico, vi or something else.

3. Press ⏎Enter.

tin: Starting tin

To read any of these newsgroups, you must subscribe to them. The list of newsgroups is everchanging and every time you start tin, you will be asked if you want to subscribe to any of the newsgroups that have appeared since the last time you ran tin.

To start tin:

1. Type **tin**.

2. Press 〔↵Enter〕.

3. (Optional) If there are new newsgroups available, tin will ask you whether you want to subscribe each one.

At each one, you have the option of typing one of the following:

  y to subscribe to the new group.

  n to not subscribe to this group.

  q to stop the questions and get on with reading the news.

You will then see a screen that looks like this:

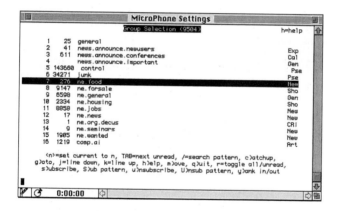

uudecode

Converts an encoded text file back to binary.

Since Internet mail can't contain binary files, you need to convert binary files to text and then include them in the message. If you've received a uuencoded binary file, you must convert it back. When someone sends you an encoded file that contains the latest cool shareware utility, this is how you decode it.

To decode a text file:

1. Type **uudecode**.

2. Press [Spacebar] and type the name of the file to decode.

3. Press [⏎Enter].

The decoded file will appear in your current directory.

uuencode

Converts a binary file to an encoded text file.

If you have the latest cool shareware utility and want to e-mail it to your friends, you have to encode it as text before you can attach it in an e-mail message.

To encode a binary file:

1. Type uuencode.

2. Press [Spacebar] and type the name of the file you want to encode.

3. Press [Spacebar] and type >.

4. Type the name you want the encoded file to have.

5. Press [⏎Enter].

vi

Edits a text file.

If you can use another editor, like pico, do so. Unless you've grown up with vi, you probably won't find the merits in it. Admittedly, many Unix programmers still like it because they can do lots of things with only a few keystrokes. However, easy to use it is not.

vi has two states of operation: inserting text and executing commands. Being user-hostile, there is no indicator to tell you which mode you are in. Pressing the Escape key (Esc) always puts you in command mode. If you type and it appears in the file, you are in input mode. Typing while you are in command mode puts you in input mode.

vi: Deleting Text

In vi, you don't just select text and delete it. That would be too easy. vi works with the concept of units of text. You specify how many units of text you want to delete using a command. To delete text:

1. Press Esc to ensure you are in command mode.

2. Move the cursor using the directional j, k, h, or l keys to where you want to delete.

3. Type one of the following commands:

   x to delete the character to the right of the cursor.

   X to delete the character to the left of the cursor (backspace).

   dd to delete the entire line.

   D to delete from the cursor to the end of the line.

   dunit where unit is one of those listed in the following table. This will delete the appropriate unit.

Unit	What It Deletes
w	To the beginning of the next word, not including punctuation.
W	To the beginning of the next word, including punctuation.
$	To the end of the current line.
G	To the end of the file.
1G	To the beginning of the file.

You can add a repeat count to the unit if you like. So typing d4w would delete four words. As you can see, this is very powerful, but also exceedingly dangerous. You can undo an action by typing **u** in command mode.

vi: Inserting Text

To insert text, you must go into input mode. You can go into insert mode in several ways.

1. Type (Esc) to ensure you are in command mode.

2. Move the cursor with the directional j, k, h, or l keys to where you want to insert.

3. Type one of the following characters:

   i to insert text before the cursor.

   a to insert text after the cursor.

   A to insert text after the end of the line.

   0 to insert text on a new line in front of the cursor.

4. Type the text you want to enter.

vi: Moving Around Files

Not only is a mouse not allowed, but the arrow keys don't even work. You need to remember a bunch of commands for moving the cursor around.

To move around:

1. Press (Esc) to get into command mode.

2. Use one of the following commands.

Key to Type	Where It Moves the Cursor
h	Left one character.
l	Right one character (intuitive, huh? You type l for right, not left).
j	Down one line.
k	Up one line.
+	Beginning of the next line.
–	Beginning of the previous line.
G	End of the file.
1G	Beginning of the file.
⌘-f	Forward one screen.
⌘-b	Back one screen.

vi: Opening Files

To edit a file:

1. Type **vi**.

2. Press [Spacebar] and type the name of the file you want to edit.

3. Press [↵Enter].

You will see a screen that looks like this:

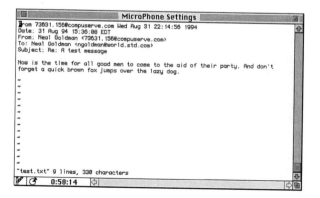

The tildes (Num Lock) indicate blank lines.

vi: Quitting vi

To exit vi and save your changes:

1. Press Esc. Your computer may beep.

2. Type **ZZ**. Make sure that they are capitalized.

To quit vi without saving any changes:

1. Press Esc. Your computer may beep.

2. Type :q!.

3. Press ↵Enter.

vi: Saving a File

To save the current file:

1. Press Esc.

2. Type :w.

3. Press ↵Enter.

WWW

Navigates the Internet using hypertext links in the the World Wide Web.

As far as the Internet is concerned, the World Wide Web is the coolest thing around. It's by far the simplest way to navigate around the Internet and explore. The World Wide Web is based on the concept of hypertext and is made up of many documents scattered around the world. Each document contains links to other documents on related topics. To follow the link, just select it and the Web takes you there. Simple. The downside (how come there's always a downside?) to WWW is that it's not great for going quickly to a specific place if you ~~~+ you want.

the Web, you use a *browser*. There are several /ill document WWW because it works on all types of computers. There is also one called lynx which does exactly the same thing, but it takes advantage of various terminal characteristics to look prettier.

To start the World Wide Web:

1. Type **www**.

2. Press ⏎Enter.

You will see a screen that looks like this:

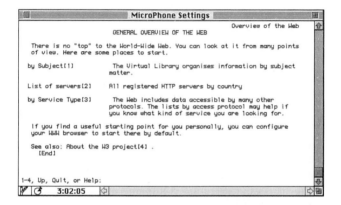

If your service doesn't have WWW, try lynx. If that doesn't work, you can telnet to a WWW server. To do that, type **telnet info.cern.ch** and press ⏎Enter. Other servers are www.njit.edu and hnsource.cc.ukans.edu (login in as www).

Topics that have links are marked by bracketed numbers, like [3].

To follow a topic:

1. Type the number of the topic you want to follow.

2. Press ⏎Enter.

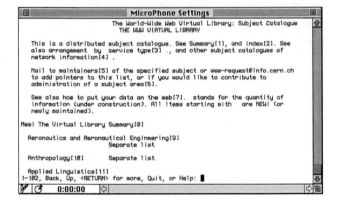

For example, if at the main screen, you type **1** and press ⏎Enter, you will be taken to the Virtual Library and see the "by Subject" listing.

There are other navigation commands as well to help you surf the web. To use one of the following commands, type the command and press ⏎Enter.

WWW Command	Action
Press ⏎Enter	Go down one page.
up	Go up one page (level).
top	Go to the first page (at top of first document).
f *keyword*	Find a keyword. Only works if you see FIND on the bottom line.
back	Go to the previous document.

WWW Command	Action
recall	List the documents you've been to already.
r *number*	Go to that document number in the recall list.
list	List all the documents that are referenced by the current document.

WWW: Saving a Document to a File

To save the text of a document you are reading:

1. Type >.

2. Press [Spacebar] and type the name you want the file to be called.

3. Press [↵Enter].

Appendix A

The Internet through America Online and CompuServe

While the Internet was founded by noncommercial groups, let it never be said that the lure of supply and demand does not apply to the Internet. Most people on the Internet today are using dial-up or direct connections to UNIX machines, but the big online services are struggling to get into the money. CompuServe, America Online, Prodigy, and Delphi all have claimed to be fully supporting Internet access by the end of 1994.

In this appendix, you'll see how to access the Internet through two of the most popular systems: America Online and CompuServe.

America Online

America Online offers both newsgroup access and a unique interface to gopher and WAIS. The interface is exactly like the other aspects of the America Online services so you should have no trouble using their Internet services.

America Online: Getting to Newsgroups

To find the newsgroup reader:

1. Pull down the **Go To** menu and select **Keyword**.

2. In the Keyword dialog box, type **Internet**.

3. Press ⏎Enter or click on **OK**.

4. Click on the **Newsgroup** icon.

America Online: Managing Your Subscription List

Like all the other newsreaders, with America Online, you need to subscribe to a newsgroup before you can read any articles in it.

To subscribe to a newsgroup when you don't know its name:

1. Click on **Newsgroups** in the Internet Center dialog box.

2. Click on the **Add Newsgroups** icon.

3. Click on a category that you think will have the newsgroup you want.

4. Click on **List Topics**.

5. Click on the category you want and click on **List newsgroups**.

6. Click on the newsgroup you want and click on **Add**.

7. Click on **OK** to add this newsgroup to your subscription list. Then click on **OK** in the confirmation box.

Okay, I fibbed. You can actually read newsgroups here, not just add them. This is good if you want to preview a newsgroup before subscribing. If you expect to read this newsgroup more than once, you will be better off subscribing to it.

To subscribe to a newsgroup if you know its name:

1. At the Newsgroup center, click on **Expert Add**.

2. In the Expert Add dialog box, type the name of the newsgroup.

3. Press ⏎Enter.

4. Click on **OK** to add this newsgroup to your subscription list. Then click on **OK** in the confirmation box.

To unsubscribe to a newsgroup:

1. At the Newsgroup center, click on the **Read My Newsgroups** icon.

2. Select the newsgroup to which you want to unsubscribe by clicking on it.

3. Press the **Remove** button.

America Online: Marking Messages as Read

Once you have read an article, it will disappear from your list. With America Online, however, you cannot mark an individual message as read. You must mark all the messages in the thread list.

To mark all the messages in a newsgroup as read:

1. Click on the **Update All as Read** icon.

2. Click on **OK** in the confirmation dialog box.

3. Click on **OK** in the acknowledgment dialog box.

America Online: Posting a New Message

To create an entirely new message thread:

1. Press the **Send a New Message** icon. A dialog box will appear.

2. Click in the **Subject** field and type in your subject heading.

3. Click in the **Message** field and type in your message.

4. Press **Send**.

America Online: Posting a Response

To respond to a message in a thread that you are reading:

1. Press the **Send Response** button. A dialog box will appear.

2. Click in the **Subject** field and edit your subject heading.

3. Click in the message field and type in your response. America Online automatically inserts a note at the top of the response so you can refer to the previous message in the thread.

4. Press **Send**.

America Online: Reading Articles

To read an article in a newsgroup, you must navigate through your list of newsgroups and then through a list of articles in the newsgroup. American Online organizes articles as lists of related subject listings called *threads*. Threads make it easy to follow a discussion on a particular topic.

To read an article:

1. At the Newsgroup center, click on the **Read My Newsgroups** icon.

2. In the newsgroup list, navigate to the newsgroup that contains articles you want to read.

3. Double-click on it or press **List Unread Subjects**. You will now be in the thread list for that newsgroup.

4. Click on the thread that contains articles that have a subject you want to explore.

5. Click on **Read Messages**. You will now be reading the first article in the thread.

6. (Optional) To move through articles in the thread, click on the **Previous** and **Next** buttons.

If you don't want to start with the first article in the thread, you can click on **List Messages** in step 3. You will see a list of the messages in the thread. Double-click on the one you want to read.

America Online: Using Gopher and WAIS

America Online has combined access to gopher and WAIS into their typical list interface where you see a list of items and choose one by double-clicking on it.

To access gopher and WAIS:

1. Pull down the **Go To** menu and select **Keyword**.

2. In the Keyword dialog box, type `Internet`.

3. Press ⏎Enter or press **OK**.

4. Click on the **Gopher & WAIS Databases** icon.

You will see a list of items, each of which corresponds to some item to be found in gopherspace or in WAIS. Double-clicking on an item will choose it. Each item has an icon to the left of it. The icon indicates what will happen when you double-click.

Icon	What Happens When You Double-Click
Folder	Another list of items to click on will appear.
File	The text file will be retrieved and displayed.
Open book	Initiates a search via WAIS.

To initiate a Veronica search using America Online:

1. Click on the **Search All Gophers** icon.

2. Type in a keyword for which you want to search.

3. Press ⏎Enter.

CompuServe

As of September, 1994, newsgroup reading was new to CompuServe and had not had much testing in volume. While the interface is not likely to change, other changes may occur over time. Newsgroup reading is part of CompuServe's extended services.

CompuServe: Getting to the Newsreader

There is currently no way to find the USENET newsreader through the icons provided in the various CompuServe Information Managers (CIMs). You must know the keyword.

To get to the USENET Newsreader.

1. Pull down the **Services** menu and select **Go**.

2. In the Transfer to Service dialog box, type **usenet**.

3. Press ⏎Enter or click **Go**.

4. Choose **USENET Newsreader (CIM)** or **USENET Newsreader**.

You will then see a screen that looks like this:

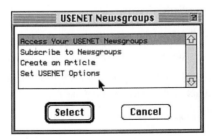

Tip

There are slight differences between the text interface and the CIM interface. The organization is close enough that these instructions should work for either interface.

CompuServe: Managing Your Subscription List

While CompuServe doesn't subscribe to all the newsgroups, such as the steamier alt.* or regional ones, there are still many to deal with. Your best bet is to create a list of newsgroups that you generally want to read.

To subscribe to a newsgroup:

1. Choose the **Subscribe to Newsgroups** menu item.

2. At the next dialog box, you can choose a newsgroup one of three ways:

3. Double-click on items in the **Browse** section until you find the name of a newsgroup to which you want to subscribe.

4. Search by name for a newsgroup by typing the string to search from in the **Keyword** field.

5. Subscribe to a specific group by name, by clicking on **Subscribe by Name** and typing in the specific newsgroup name.

6. Click on **Subscribe**.

To unsubscribe to a newsgroup:

1. Choose **Access your Newsgroups** item.

2. Select the newsgroup to which you want to unsubscribe by clicking on it.

3. Press the **Remove** button.

CompuServe: Marking Messages as Read

Once you have read an article, it will disappear from your list. However, with a few well-chosen mouse clicks, you can make messages disappear without reading them. You could be the next David Copperfield.

➤ To mark an article as read, press the **Clear** button.

➤ To mark an article as unread, press the **Reread** button.

CompuServe: Posting a New Message

To create an entirely new message thread:

1. Press the **Create** button. A dialog box will appear.

2. Click in the **Subject** field and type in your subject heading.

3. Click in the message field and type in your message.

4. Press **Send**.

CompuServe: Posting a Response

To respond to a message in a thread that you are reading:

1. Press the **Reply** button. A dialog box will appear.

2. Click in the **Subject** field and edit your subject heading.

3. Click in the message field and type in your response. Be as witty as possible.

4. Press **Send**.

To respond by e-mail directly to the person who posted the message, rather than back to the newsgroup, select the e-mail check box, rather than the post to newsgroup check box.

CompuServe: Reading Articles

To read an article in a newsgroup, you must navigate through your list of newsgroups and then through a list of articles in the newsgroup. CompuServe organizes articles as lists of related subject listings called threads. Threads make it easy to follow a discussion on a particular topic.

To read an article:

1. In the newsgroup list, navigate to the newsgroup that contains articles you want to read.

2. Double-click on it or press **Browse**. You will now be in the thread list for that newsgroup.

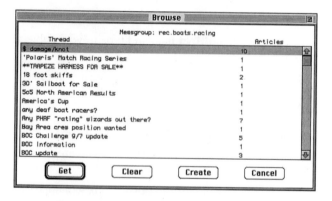

3. Click on the thread that contains articles that have a subject you want to explore.

The numbers next to the thread indicate the number of articles in that thread.

4. Click on **Get**. You will now be reading the first article in the thread.

5. (Optional) To move through articles in the thread, click on the > and < buttons. To move to the next thread, click on the **Next** button.

Appendix B

USENET Newsgroups

Okay, so you're probably thinking, "What now? What mischief can I get into on the Internet, now that I know how to use it?" Glad you asked. USENET newsgroups are an excellent place to start. You can make your opinion known on a staggering variety of subjects.

USENET Newsgroup Classifications

The USENET newsgroups divide into seven categories:

comp	Topics of interest to both computer professionals and hobbyists, including topics in computer science, software source, and information on hardware and software systems.
sci	Discussions marked by special, and usually practical, knowledge relating to research in or application of the established sciences.
misc	Groups addressing themes not easily classified under any of the other headings or that incorporate themes from multiple categories.
soc	Groups primarily addressing social issues and socializing.
talk	Groups largely debate-oriented and tending to feature long discussions without resolution and without appreciable amounts of generally useful information.
news	Groups concerned with the news network and software themselves.
rec	Groups oriented towards the arts, hobbies, and recreational activities.

USENET Groups (By Category)

Newsgroup	Description
comp.admin.policy	Discussions of site administration policies.
comp.ai	Artificial intelligence discussions.
comp.ai.alife	Research about artificial life.
comp.ai.fuzzy	Fuzzy set theory, aka fuzzy logic.
comp.ai.genetic	Genetic algorithms in computing.
comp.ai.jair.announce	Announcements and abstracts of the Journal of AI Research.
comp.ai.jair.papers	Papers published by the Journal of AI Research.
comp.ai.nat-lang	Natural language processing by computers.
comp.ai.neural-nets	All aspects of neural networks.
comp.ai.nlang-know-rep	Natural Language and Knowledge Representation.
comp.ai.philosophy	Philosophical aspects of artificial Intelligence.
comp.ai.shells	Artificial intelligence applied to shells.
comp.answers	Repository for periodic USENET articles.
comp.apps.spreadsheets	Spreadsheets on various platforms.
comp.arch	Computer architecture.
comp.arch.arithmetic	Implementing arithmetic on computers/digital systems.
comp.arch.bus.vmebus	Hardware and software for VMEbus Systems.
comp.arch.fpga	Field Programmable Gate Array based computing systems.
comp.arch.storage	Storage system issues, both hardware and software.

Newsgroup	Description
comp.archives	Descriptions of public access archives.
comp.archives. admin	Issues relating to computer archive administration.
comp.archives. msdos.announce	Announcements about MS-DOS archives.
comp.archives. msdos.d	Discussion of materials available in MS-DOS archives.
comp.bbs.misc	All aspects of computer bulletin board systems.
comp.bbs.tbbs	The Bread Board System bulletin board software.
comp.bbs.waffle	The Waffle BBS and USENET system on all platforms.
comp.benchmarks	Discussion of benchmarking techniques and results.
comp.binaries.acorn	Binary-only postings for Acorn machines.
comp.binaries.amiga	Encoded public domain programs in binary.
comp.binaries. apple2	Binary-only postings for the Apple II computer.
comp.binaries. atari.st	Binary-only postings for the Atari ST.
comp.binaries.cbm	For the transfer of 8bit Commodore binaries.
comp.binaries.geos	Binaries for the GEOS operating system.
comp.binaries. ibm.pc	Binary-only postings for IBM PC/ MS-DOS.
comp.binaries.ibm. pc.d	Discussions about IBM/PC binary postings.
comp.binaries.ibm. pc.wanted	Requests for IBM PC and compatible programs.

Newsgroup	Description
comp.binaries.mac	Encoded Macintosh programs in binary.
comp.binaries.ms-windows	Binary programs for Microsoft Windows.
comp.binaries.newton	Apple Newton binaries, sources, books, etc.
comp.binaries.os2	Binaries for use under the OS/2 ABI.
comp.bugs.2bsd	Reports of UNIX* version 2BSD related bugs.
comp.bugs.4bsd	Reports of UNIX version 4BSD related bugs.
comp.bugs.4bsd.ucb-fixes	Bug reports/fixes for BSD Unix.
comp.bugs.misc	General UNIX bug reports and fixes (incl V7, uucp).
comp.bugs.sys5	Reports of USG (System III, V, etc.) bugs.
comp.cad.cadence	Users of Cadence Design Systems products.
comp.cad.compass	Compass Design Automation EDA tools.
comp.cad.pro-engineer	Parametric Technology's Pro/Engineer design package.
comp.cad.synthesis	Research and production in the field of logic synthesis.
comp.client-server	Topics relating to client/server technology.
comp.cog-eng	Cognitive engineering.
comp.compilers	Compiler construction, theory, etc.
comp.compilers.tools.pccts	Construction of compilers and tools with PCCTS.

Newsgroup	Description
comp.compression	Data compression algorithms and theory.
comp.compression.research	Discussions about data compression research.
comp.constraints	Constraint processing and related topics.
comp.databases	Database and data management issues and theory.
comp.databases.informix	Informix database management software discussions.
comp.databases.ingres	Issues relating to INGRES products.
comp.databases.ms-access	MS Windows' relational database system, Access.
comp.databases.object	Object-oriented paradigms in database systems.
comp.databases.oracle	The SQL database products of the Oracle Corporation.
comp.databases.paradox	Borland's database for DOS & MS Windows.
comp.databases.pick	Pick-like, post-relational, database systems.
comp.databases.rdb	The relational database engine RDB from DEC.
comp.databases.sybase	Implementations of the SQL Server.
comp.databases.theory	Discussing advances in database technology.
comp.databases.xbase.fox	Fox Software's xBase system and compatibles.
comp.databases.xbase.misc	Discussion of xBase (dBASE-like) products.
comp.dcom.cabling	Cabling selection, installation and use.

Newsgroup	Description
comp.dcom. cell-relay	Forum for discussion of Cell Relay-based products.
comp.dcom.fax	Fax hardware, software, and protocols.
comp.dcom.isdn	The Integrated Services Digital Network (ISDN).
comp.dcom.lans. ethernet	Discussions of the Ethernet/IEEE 802.3 protocols.
comp.dcom. lans.fddi	Discussions of the FDDI protocol suite.
comp.dcom. lans.misc	Local area network hardware and software.
comp.dcom.lans. token-ring	Installing and using token ring networks.
comp.dcom. modems	Data communications hardware and software.
comp.dcom.servers	Selecting and operating data communications servers.
comp.dcom. sys.cisco	Info on Cisco routers and bridges.
comp.dcom.sys. wellfleet	Wellfleet bridge & router systems hardware & software.
comp.dcom.telecom	Telecommunications digest.
comp.dcom. telecom.tech	Discussion of technical aspects of telephony.
comp.doc	Archived public-domain documentation.
comp.doc. techreports	Lists of technical reports.
comp.dsp	Digital Signal Processing using computers.
comp.edu	Computer science education.
comp.edu. languages.natural	Computer assisted languages instruction issues.

Newsgroup	Description
comp.emacs	EMACS editors of different flavors.
comp.emulators. announce	Emulator news, FAQs, announcements.
comp.emulators. apple2	Emulators of Apple // systems.
comp.emulators. cbm	Emulators of C-64, C-128, PET, and VIC-20 systems.
comp.emulators. misc	Emulators of miscellaneous computer systems.
comp.emulators. ms-windows.wine	A free MS-Windows emulator under X.
comp.fonts	Typefonts — design, conversion, use, etc.
comp.graphics	Computer graphics, art, animation, image processing.
comp.graphics. algorithms	Algorithms used in producing computer graphics.
comp.graphics. animation	Technical aspects of computer animation.
comp.graphics.avs	The Application Visualization System.
comp.graphics. data-explorer	IBM's Visualization Data Explorer, aka DX.
comp.graphics. explorer	The Explorer Modular Visualisation Environment (MVE).
comp.graphics. gnuplot	The GNUPLOT interactive function plotter.
comp.graphics. opengl	The OpenGL 3D application programming interface.
comp.graphics. raytracing	Ray tracing software, tools, and methods.
comp.graphics. research	Highly technical computer graphics discussion.

Newsgroup	Description
comp.graphics. visualization	Info on scientific visualization.
comp.groupware	Software and hardware for shared interactive environments.
comp.groupware. lotus-notes.misc	Lotus Notes related discussions.
comp.home. automation	Home automation devices, setup, sources, etc.
comp.home.misc	Media, technology and information in domestic spaces.
comp.human-factors	Issues related to human-computer interaction (HCI).
comp.infosystems	Any discussion about information systems.
comp.infosystems. announce	Announcements of internet information services.
comp. infosystems.gis	All aspects of Geographic Information Systems.
comp.infosystems. gopher	Discussion of the Gopher information service.
comp.infosystems. interpedia	The Internet Encyclopedia.
comp.infosystems. kiosks	Information kiosks.
comp.infosystems. wais	The Z39.50-based WAIS full-text search system.
comp.infosystems. www	The World Wide Web information system.
comp.infosystems. www.misc	Miscellaneous World Wide Web discussion.
comp.infosystems. www.providers	WWW provider issues (info providers).
comp.infosystems. www.users	WWW user issues (Mosaic, Lynx, etc).

Newsgroup	Description
comp.internet.library	Discussing electronic libraries.
comp.ivideodisc	Interactive videodiscs—uses, potential, etc.
comp.lang.ada	Discussion about Ada*.
comp.lang.apl	Discussion about APL.
comp.lang.basic.misc	Other dialects and aspects of BASIC.
comp.lang.basic.visual	Microsoft Visual Basic & App Basic; Windows & DOS.
comp.lang.c	Discussion about C.
comp.lang.c++	The object-oriented C++ language.
comp.lang.clos	Common Lisp Object System discussions.
comp.lang.dylan	For discussion of the Dylan language.
comp.lang.eiffel	The object-oriented Eiffel language.
comp.lang.forth	Discussion about Forth.
comp.lang.fortran	Discussion about FORTRAN.
comp.lang.functional	Discussion about functional languages.
comp.lang.hermes	The Hermes language for distributed applications.
comp.lang.idl-pvwave	IDL and PV-Wave language discussions.
comp.lang.lisp	Discussion about LISP.
comp.lang.lisp.mcl	Discussing Apple's Macintosh Common Lisp.
comp.lang.logo	The Logo teaching and learning language.

Newsgroup	Description
comp.lang.misc	Different computer languages not specifically listed.
comp.lang.ml	ML languages including Standard ML, CAML, Lazy ML, etc.
comp.lang.modula2	Discussion about Modula-2.
comp.lang.modula3	Discussion about the Modula-3 language.
comp.lang.mumps	The M (MUMPS) language & technology, in general.
comp.lang.oberon	The Oberon language and system.
comp.lang.objective-c	The Objective-C language and environment.
comp.lang.pascal	Discussion about Pascal.
comp.lang.perl	Discussion of Larry Wall's Perl system.
comp.lang.pop	Pop11 and the Plug user group.
comp.lang.postscript	The PostScript Page Description Language.
comp.lang.prograph	Prograph, a visual object-oriented dataflow language.
comp.lang.prolog	Discussion about PROLOG.
comp.lang.python	The Python computer language.
comp.lang.sather	The object-oriented computer language Sather.
comp.lang.scheme	The Scheme Programming language.
comp.lang.sigplan	Info & announcements from ACM SIGPLAN.
comp.lang.smalltalk	Discussion about Smalltalk 80.
comp.lang.tcl	The Tcl programming language and related tools.
comp.lang.verilog	Discussing Verilog and PLI.

Newsgroup	Description
comp.lang.vhdl	VHSIC Hardware Description Language, IEEE 1076/87.
comp.laser-printers	Laser printers, hardware & software.
comp.lsi	Large scale integrated circuits.
comp.lsi.testing	Testing of electronic circuits.
comp.mail.elm	Discussion and fixes for the ELM mail system.
comp.mail.headers	Gatewayed from the Internet header-people list.
comp.mail.maps	Various maps, including UUCP maps.
comp.mail.mh	The UCI version of the Rand Message Handling system.
comp.mail.mime	Multipurpose Internet Mail Extensions of RFC 1341.
comp.mail.misc	General discussions about computer mail.
comp.mail.mush	The Mail User's Shell (MUSH).
comp.mail.pine	The PINE mail user agent.
comp.mail.sendmail	Configuring and using the BSD sendmail agent.
comp.mail.smail	Administering & using the smail email transport system.
comp.mail.uucp	Mail in the uucp network environment.
comp.misc	General topics about computers not covered elsewhere.
comp.multimedia	Interactive multimedia technologies of all kinds.
comp.newprod	Announcements of new products of interest.
comp.object	Object-oriented programming and languages.

Newsgroup	Description
comp.object.logic	Integrating object-oriented and logic programming.
comp.org.acm	Topics about the Association for Computing Machinery.
comp.org.cpsr. announce	Computer Professionals for Social Responsibility.
comp.org.cpsr.talk	Issues of computing and social responsibility.
comp.org.decus	Digital Equipment Computer Users' Society newsgroup.
comp.org.eff.news	News from the Electronic Frontier Foundation.
comp.org.eff.talk	Discussion of EFF goals, strategies, etc.
comp.org.fidonet	FidoNews digest, official news of FidoNet Assoc.
comp.org.ieee	Issues and announcements about the IEEE & its members.
comp.org.issnnet	The International Student Society for Neural Networks.
comp.org.lisp-users	Association of Lisp Users related discussions.
comp.org.sug	Talk about/for the The Sun User's Group.
comp.org.usenix	USENIX Association events and announcements.
comp.org.usenix. roomshare	Finding lodging during Usenix conferences.
comp.os.386bsd. announce	Announcements relating to the 386bsd operating system.
comp.os.386bsd. apps	Applications which run under 386bsd.
comp.os.386bsd. bugs	Bugs and fixes for the 386bsd OS and its clients.

Newsgroup	Description
comp.os.386bsd. development	Working on 386bsd internals.
comp.os.386bsd. misc	General aspects of 386bsd not covered by other groups.
comp.os.386bsd. questions	General questions about 386bsd.
comp.os.chorus	CHORUS microkernel issues, research and developments.
comp.os.coherent	Discussion and support of the Coherent operating system.
comp.os.cpm	Discussion about the CP/M operating system.
comp.os.geos	The GEOS operating system by GeoWorks for PC clones.
comp.os.linux. admin	Installing and administering Linux systems.
comp.os.linux. announce	Announcements important to the Linux community.
comp.os.linux. development	Ongoing work on the Linux operating system.
comp.os.linux.help	Questions and advice about Linux.
comp.os.linux.misc	Linux-specific topics not covered by other groups.
comp.os.lynx	Discussion of LynxOS and Lynx Real-Time Systems.
comp.os.mach	The MACH OS from CMU & other places.
comp.os.minix	Discussion of Tanenbaum's MINIX system.
comp.os.misc	General OS-oriented discussion not carried elsewhere.
comp.os. ms-windows. advocacy	Speculation and debate about Microsoft Windows.

Newsgroup	Description
comp.os. ms-windows. announce	Announcements relating to Windows.
comp.os. ms-windows.apps	Applications in the Windows environment.
comp.os. ms-windows.apps. comm	MS-Windows communication applications.
comp.os. ms-windows.apps. financial	MS-Windows financial & tax software.
comp.os. ms-windows. apps.misc	MS-Windows applications.
comp.os. ms-windows. apps.utilities	MS-Windows utilities.
comp.os. ms-windows. apps.word-proc	MS-Windows word-processing applications.
comp.os. ms-windows.misc	General discussions about Windows issues.
comp.os. ms-windows. networking.misc	Windows and other networks.
comp.os. ms-windows. networking.tcp-ip	Windows and TCP/IP networking.
comp.os. ms-windows. networking.windows	Windows' built-in networking.
comp.os.m s-windows.nt.misc	General discussion about Windows NT.
comp.os. ms-windows. nt.setup	Configuring Windows NT systems.

Newsgroup	Description
comp.os. ms-windows. programmer.controls	Controls, dialogs and VBXs.
comp.os. ms-windows. programmer.drivers	Win16/Win32 drivers and VxDs.
comp.os. ms-windows. programmer.graphics	GDI, graphics, and printing.
comp.os. ms-windows. programmer.memory	Memory management issues.
comp.os. ms-windows. programmer.misc	Programming Microsoft Windows.
comp.os. ms-windows. programmer. multimedia	Multimedia programming.
comp.os. ms-windows. programmer.networks	Network programming.
comp.os. ms-windows. programmer.ole	OLE2, COM, and DDE programming.
comp.os. ms-windows. programmer.tools	Development tools in Windows.
comp.os. ms-windows. programmer.win32	32-bit Windows programming interfaces.
comp.os. ms-windows. programmer.winhelp	WinHelp/Multimedia Viewer development.
comp.os. ms-windows.setup	Installing and configuring Microsoft Windows.

Newsgroup	Description
comp.os.ms-windows.video	Video adapters and drivers for Windows.
comp.os.msdos.apps	Discussion of applications that run under MS-DOS.
comp.os.msdos.desqview	QuarterDeck's Desqview and related products.
comp.os.msdos.mail-news	Administering mail & network news systems under MS-DOS.
comp.os.msdos.misc	Miscellaneous topics about MS-DOS machines.
comp.os.msdos.pcgeos	GeoWorks PC/GEOS and PC/GEOS-based packages.
comp.os.msdos.programmer	Programming MS-DOS machines.
comp.os.msdos.programmer.turbovision	Borland's text application libraries.
comp.os.os2.advocacy	Supporting and flaming OS/2.
comp.os.os2.announce	Notable news and announcements related to OS/2.
comp.os.os2.apps	Discussions of applications under OS/2.
comp.os.os2.beta	All aspects of beta releases of OS/2 systems software.
comp.os.os2.bugs	OS/2 system bug reports, fixes, and work-arounds.
comp.os.os2.games	Running games under OS/2.
comp.os.os2.misc	Miscellaneous topics about the OS/2 system.
comp.os.os2.multimedia	Multimedia on OS/2 systems.
comp.os.os2.networking.misc	Miscellaneous networking issues of OS/2.

Newsgroup	Description
comp.os.os2.networking.tcp-ip	TCP/IP under OS/2.
comp.os.os2.programmer.misc	Programming OS/2 machines.
comp.os.os2.programmer.oop	Programming system objects (SOM, WPS, etc).
comp.os.os2.programmer.porting	Porting software to OS/2 machines.
comp.os.os2.programmer.tools	Compilers, assemblers, interpreters under OS/2.
comp.os.os2.setup	Installing and configuring OS/2 systems.
comp.os.os9	Discussions about the os9 operating system.
comp.os.parix	Forum for users of the parallel operating system PARIX.
comp.os.qnx	Using and developing under the QNX operating system.
comp.os.research	Operating systems and related areas.
comp.os.vms	DEC's VAX* line of computers & VMS.
comp.os.vxworks	The VxWorks real-time operating system.
comp.os.xinu	The XINU operating system from Purdue (D. Comer).
comp.parallel	Massively parallel hardware/software.
comp.parallel.mpi	Message Passing Interface (MPI).
comp.parallel.pvm	The PVM system of multi-computer parallelization.
comp.patents	Discussing patents of computer technology.
comp.periphs	Peripheral devices.

Newsgroup	Description
comp.periphs.scsi	Discussion of SCSI-based peripheral devices.
comp.programming	Programming issues that transcend languages and OSs.
comp.programming. literate	Literate programs and programming tools.
comp.protocols. appletalk	Applebus hardware & software.
comp.protocols. dicom	Digital Imaging and Communications in Medicine.
comp.protocols.ibm	Networking with IBM mainframes.
comp.protocols.iso	The ISO protocol stack.
comp.protocols. kerberos	The Kerberos authentication server.
comp.protocols. kermit	Info about the Kermit package.
comp.protocols. misc	Various forms and types of protocol.
comp.protocols.nfs	Discussion about the Network File System protocol.
comp.protocols.ppp	Discussion of the Internet Point to Point Protocol.
comp.protocols. tcp-ip	TCP and IP network protocols.
comp.protocols. tcp-ip.ibmpc	TCP/IP for IBM(-like) personal computers.
comp.publish. cdrom.hardware	Hardware used in publishing with CD-ROM.
comp.publish. cdrom.multimedia	Software for multimedia authoring & publishing.
comp.publish. cdrom.software	Software used in publishing with CD-ROM.

Newsgroup	Description
comp.publish. prepress	Electronic prepress.
comp.realtime	Issues related to real-time computing.
comp.research. japan	The nature of research in Japan.
comp.risks	Risks to the public from computers & users.
comp.robotics	All aspects of robots and their applications.
comp.security.misc	Security issues of computers and networks.
comp.security.unix	Discussion of Unix security.
comp.simulation	Simulation methods, problems, uses.
comp.society	The impact of technology on society.
comp.society. cu-digest	The Computer Underground Digest.
comp.society. development	Computer technology in developing countries.
comp.society. folklore	Computer folklore & culture, past & present.
comp.society. futures	Events in technology affecting future computing.
comp.society. privacy	Effects of technology on privacy.
comp.soft-sys. khoros	The Khoros X11 visualization system.
comp.soft-sys. matlab	The MathWorks calculation and visualization package.
comp.soft-sys. powerbuilder	Application development tools from PowerSoft.

Newsgroup	Description
comp.soft-sys. ptolemy	The Ptolemy simulation/code generation environment.
comp.soft-sys.sas	The SAS statistics package.
comp.soft-sys. shazam	The SHAZAM econometrics computer program.
comp.soft-sys.spss	The SPSS statistics package.
comp.soft-sys. wavefront	Wavefront software products, problems, etc.
comp.software-eng	Software Engineering and related topics.
comp.software. config-mgmt	Configuration management, tools, and procedures.
comp.software. international	Finding, using, & writing non-English software.
comp.software. licensing	Software licensing technology.
comp.software. testing	All aspects of testing computer systems.
comp.sources.3b1	Source code-only postings for the AT&T 3b1.
comp.sources. acorn	Source code-only postings for the Acorn.
comp.sources. amiga	Source code-only postings for the Amiga.
comp.sources. apple2	Source code and discussion for the Apple2.
comp.sources. atari.st	Source code-only postings for the Atari ST.
comp.sources.bugs	Bug reports, fixes, discussion for posted sources.
comp.sources.d	For any discussion of source postings.
comp.sources. games	Postings of recreational software.

Newsgroup	Description
comp.sources.games.bugs	Bug reports and fixes for posted game software.
comp.sources.hp48	Programs for the HP48 and HP28 calculators.
comp.sources.mac	Software for the Apple Macintosh.
comp.sources.misc	Posting of software.
comp.sources.postscript	Source code for programs written in PostScript.
comp.sources.reviewed	Source code evaluated by peer review.
comp.sources.sun	Software for Sun workstations.
comp.sources.testers	Finding people to test software.
comp.sources.unix	Postings of complete, UNIX-oriented sources.
comp.sources.wanted	Requests for software and fixes.
comp.sources.x	Software for the X windows system.
comp.specification	Languages and methodologies for formal specification.
comp.specification.z	Discussion about the formal specification notation Z.
comp.speech	Research & applications in speech science & technology.
comp.std.c	Discussion about C language standards.
comp.std.c++	Discussion about C++ language, library, standards.
comp.std.internat	Discussion about international standards.
comp.std.lisp	User group (ALU) supported standards.

Newsgroup	Description
comp.std.misc	Discussion about various standards.
comp.std.mumps	Discussion for the X11.1 committee on Mumps.
comp.std.unix	Discussion for the P1003 committee on UNIX.
comp.std.wireless	Examining standards for wireless network technology.
comp.sw.components	Software components and related technology.
comp.sys.3b1	Discussion and support of AT&T 7300/3B1/UnixPC.
comp.sys.acorn	Discussion on Acorn and ARM-based computers.
comp.sys.acorn.advocacy	Why Acorn computers and programs are better.
comp.sys.acorn.announce	Announcements for Acorn and ARM users.
comp.sys.acorn.games	Discussion of games for Acorn machines.
comp.sys.acorn.tech	Software and hardware aspects of Acorn and ARM products.
comp.sys.alliant	Info and discussion about Alliant computers.
comp.sys.amiga.advocacy	Why an Amiga is better than XYZ.
comp.sys.amiga.announce	Announcements about the Amiga.
comp.sys.amiga.applications	Miscellaneous applications.
comp.sys.amiga.audio	Music, MIDI, speech synthesis, other sounds.
comp.sys.amiga.cd32	Technical and computing talk for Commodore Amiga CD32.

Newsgroup	Description
comp.sys.amiga.datacomm	Methods of getting bytes in and out.
comp.sys.amiga.emulations	Various hardware & software emulators.
comp.sys.amiga.games	Discussion of games for the Commodore Amiga.
comp.sys.amiga.graphics	Charts, graphs, pictures, etc.
comp.sys.amiga.hardware	Amiga computer hardware, Q&A, reviews, etc.
comp.sys.amiga.introduction	Group for newcomers to Amigas.
comp.sys.amiga.marketplace	Where to find it, prices, etc.
comp.sys.amiga.misc	Discussions not falling in another Amiga group.
comp.sys.amiga.multimedia	Animations, video, & multimedia.
comp.sys.amiga.networking	Amiga networking software/hardware.
comp.sys.amiga.programmer	Developers & hobbyists discuss code.
comp.sys.amiga.reviews	Reviews of Amiga software, hardware.
comp.sys.amiga.uucp	Amiga UUCP packages.
comp.sys.apollo	Apollo computer systems.
comp.sys.apple2	Discussion about Apple II micros.
comp.sys.apple2.comm	Apple II data communications.
comp.sys.apple2.gno	The AppleIIgs GNO multitasking environment.
comp.sys.apple2.marketplace	Buying, selling, and trading Apple II equipment.

Newsgroup	Description
comp.sys.apple2. programmer	Programming on the Apple II.
comp.sys.apple2. usergroups	All about Apple II user groups.
comp.sys.atari.8bit	Discussion about 8 bit Atari micros.
comp.sys.atari. advocacy	Attacking and defending Atari computers.
comp.sys.atari. announce	Atari related hard/software announcements.
comp.sys.atari.st	Discussion about 16 bit Atari micros.
comp.sys.atari. st.tech	Technical discussions of Atari ST hard/software.
comp.sys.att	Discussions about AT&T micro-computers.
comp.sys.cbm	Discussion about Commodore micros.
comp.sys. concurrent	The Concurrent/Masscomp line of computers.
comp.sys.convex	Convex computer systems hardware and software.
comp.sys.dec	Discussions about DEC computer systems.
comp.sys.dec.micro	DEC Micros (Rainbow, Professional 350/380)
comp.sys.encore	Encore's MultiMax computers.
comp.sys.harris	Harris computer systems, especially real-time systems.
comp.sys.hp.apps	Discussion of software and apps on all HP platforms.
comp.sys.hp. hardware	Discussion of Hewlett-Packard system hardware.

Newsgroup	Description
comp.sys.hp.hpux	Issues pertaining to HP-UX & 9000 series computers.
comp.sys.hp.misc	Issues not covered in any other comp.sys.hp.* group.
comp.sys.hp.mpe	Issues pertaining to MPE & 3000 series computers.
comp.sys.hp48	Hewlett-Packard's HP48 and HP28 calculators.
comp.sys.ibm. pc.demos	Demonstration programs which showcase programmer skill.
comp.sys.ibm. pc.digest	The IBM PC, PC-XT, and PC-AT.
comp.sys.ibm.pc. games.action	Arcade-style games on PCs.
comp.sys.ibm.pc. games.adventure	Adventure (non-rpg) games on PCs.
comp.sys.ibm.pc. games.announce	Announcements for all PC gamers.
comp.sys.ibm.pc. games.flight-sim	Flight simulators on PCs.
comp.sys.ibm.pc. games.misc	Games not covered by other PC groups.
comp.sys.ibm.pc. games.rpg	Role-playing games on the PC.
comp.sys.ibm.pc. games.strategic	Strategy/planning games on PCs.
comp.sys.ibm.pc. hardware.cd-rom	CD-ROM drives and interfaces for the PC.
comp.sys.ibm.pc. hardware.chips	Processor, cache, memory chips, etc.
comp.sys.ibm.pc. hardware.comm	Modems & communication cards for the PC.
comp.sys.ibm.pc. hardware.misc	Miscellaneous PC hardware topics.

Newsgroup	Description
comp.sys.ibm.pc. hardware. networking	Network hardware & equipment for the PC.
comp.sys.ibm.pc. hardware.storage	Hard drives & other PC storage devices.
comp.sys.ibm.pc. hardware.systems	Whole IBM PC computer & clone systems.
comp.sys.ibm.pc.	Video cards & monitors for the PC.
comp.sys.ibm. pc.misc	Discussion about IBM personal computers.
comp.sys.ibm.pc.rt	Topics related to IBM's RT computer.
comp.sys.ibm.pc. soundcard	Hardware and software aspects of PC sound cards.
comp.sys.ibm.pc. soundcard.advocacy	Advocacy for a particular soundcard.
comp.sys.ibm.pc. soundcard.games	Questions about using soundcards with games.
comp.sys.ibm.pc. soundcard.misc	Soundcards in general.
comp.sys.ibm.pc. soundcard.music	Music and sound questions using soundcards.
comp.sys.ibm.pc. soundcard.tech	Technical questions about pc soundcards.
comp.sys.ibm. ps2.hardware	Microchannel hardware, any vendor.
comp.sys.intel	Discussions about Intel systems and parts.
comp.sys.isis	The ISIS distributed system from Cornell.
comp.sys.laptops	Laptop (portable) computers.
comp.sys.m6809	Discussion about 6809's.
comp.sys.m68k	Discussion about 68k's.

Newsgroup	Description
comp.sys.m68k.pc	Discussion about 68k-based PCs.
comp.sys.m88k	Discussion about 88k-based computers.
comp.sys.mac. advocacy	The Macintosh computer family compared to others.
comp.sys.mac. announce	Important notices for Macintosh users.
comp.sys.mac.apps	Discussions of Macintosh applications.
comp.sys.mac. comm	Discussion of Macintosh communications.
comp.sys.mac. databases	Database systems for the Apple Macintosh.
comp.sys.mac. digest	Apple Macintosh: info & uses, but no programs.
comp.sys.mac. games	Discussions of games on the Macintosh.
comp.sys.mac. graphics	Macintosh graphics: paint, draw, 3D, CAD, animation.
comp.sys.mac. hardware	Macintosh hardware issues & discussions.
comp.sys.mac. hypercard	The Macintosh Hypercard: info & uses.
comp.sys.mac.misc	General discussions about the Apple Macintosh.
comp.sys.mac.oop. macapp3	Version 3 of the MacApp object oriented system.
comp.sys.mac. oop.misc	Object oriented programming issues on the Mac.
comp.sys.mac. oop.tcl	Symantec's THINK Class Library for object programming.
comp.sys.mac. portables	Discussion particular to laptop Macintoshes.

Newsgroup	Description
comp.sys.mac. programmer	Discussion by people programming the Apple Macintosh.
comp.sys.mac. scitech	Using the Macintosh in scientific & technological work.
comp.sys.mac. system	Discussions of Macintosh system software.
comp.sys.mac. wanted	Postings of "I want XYZ for my Mac."
comp.sys.mentor	Mentor Graphics products & the Silicon Compiler System.
comp.sys.mips	Systems based on MIPS chips.
comp.sys.misc	Discussion about computers of all kinds.
comp.sys.ncr	Discussion about NCR computers.
comp.sys.newton. announce	Newton information posts.
comp.sys.newton. misc	Miscellaneous discussion about Newton systems.
comp.sys.newton. programmer	Discussion of Newton software development.
comp.sys.next. advocacy	The NeXT religion.
comp.sys.next. announce	Announcements related to the NeXT computer system.
comp.sys.next.bugs	Discussion and solutions for known NeXT bugs.
comp.sys.next. hardware	Discussing the physical aspects of NeXT computers.
comp.sys.next. marketplace	NeXT hardware, software and jobs.
comp.sys.next.misc	General discussion about the NeXT computer system.

Newsgroup	Description
comp.sys.next. programmer	NeXT related programming issues.
comp.sys.next. software	Function, use, and availability of NeXT programs.
comp.sys.next. sysadmin	Discussions related to NeXT system administration.
comp.sys.novell	Discussion of Novell Netware products.
comp.sys.nsc.32k	National Semiconductor 32000 series chips.
comp.sys.palmtops	Super-powered calculators in the palm of your hand.
comp.sys.pen	Interacting with computers through pen gestures.
comp.sys.powerpc	General PowerPC Discussion.
comp.sys.prime	Prime Computer products.
comp.sys.proteon	Proteon gateway products.
comp.sys.psion	Discussion about PSION Personal Computers & Organizers.
comp.sys.pyramid	Pyramid 90x computers.
comp.sys.ridge	Ridge 32 computers and ROS.
comp.sys.sequent	Sequent systems, (Balance and Symmetry).
comp.sys.sgi.admin	System administration on Silicon Graphics's Irises.
comp.sys.sgi. announce	Announcements for the SGI community.
comp.sys.sgi.apps	Applications which run on the Iris.
comp.sys.sgi.audio	Audio on SGI systems.
comp.sys.sgi.bugs	Bugs found in the IRIX operating system.

Newsgroup	Description
comp.sys.sgi.graphics	Graphics packages and issues on SGI machines.
comp.sys.sgi.hardware	Base systems and peripherals for Iris computers.
comp.sys.sgi.misc	General discussion about Silicon Graphics's machines.
comp.sys.sinclair	Sinclair computers, eg. the ZX81, Spectrum and QL.
comp.sys.stratus	Stratus products, incl. System/88, CPS-32, VOS, and FTX.
comp.sys.sun.admin	Sun system administration issues and questions.
comp.sys.sun.announce	Sun announcements and Sunergy mailings.
comp.sys.sun.apps	Software applications for Sun computer systems.
comp.sys.sun.hardware	Sun Microsystems hardware.
comp.sys.sun.misc	Miscellaneous discussions about Sun products.
comp.sys.sun.wanted	People looking for Sun products and support.
comp.sys.tahoe	CCI 6/32, Harris HCX/7, & Sperry 7000 computers.
comp.sys.tandy	Discussion about Tandy computers: new & old.
comp.sys.ti	Discussion about Texas Instruments.
comp.sys.transputer	The Transputer computer and OCCAM language.
comp.sys.unisys	Sperry, Burroughs, Convergent and Unisys* systems.
comp.sys.xerox	Xerox 1100 workstations and protocols.

Newsgroup	Description
comp.sys. zenith.z100	The Zenith Z-100 (Heath H-100) family of computers.
comp.terminals	All sorts of terminals.
comp.text	Text processing issues and methods.
comp.text.desktop	Technology & techniques of desktop publishing.
comp.text.frame	Desktop publishing with FrameMaker.
comp.text.interleaf	Applications and use of Interleaf software.
comp.text.sgml	ISO 8879 SGML, structured documents, markup languages.
comp.text.tex	Discussion about the TeX and LaTeX systems & macros.
comp.theory. info-retrieval	Information Retrieval topics.
comp.unix.admin	Administering a Unix-based system.
comp.unix. advocacy	Arguments for and against Unix and Unix versions.
comp.unix.aix	IBM's version of UNIX.
comp.unix.amiga	Minix, SYSV4 and other *nix on an Amiga.
comp.unix.aux	The version of UNIX for Apple Macintosh II computers.
comp.unix.bsd	Discussion of Berkeley Software Distribution UNIX.
comp.unix. dos-under-unix	MS-DOS running under UNIX by whatever means.
comp.unix.internals	Discussions on hacking UNIX internals.
comp.unix.large	UNIX on mainframes and in large networks.

Newsgroup	Description
comp.unix.misc	Various topics that don't fit other groups.
comp.unix.osf.misc	Various aspects of Open Software Foundation products.
comp.unix.osf.osf1	The Open Software Foundation's OSF/1.
comp.unix. pc-clone.16bit	UNIX on 286 architectures.
comp.unix. pc-clone.32bit	UNIX on 386 and 486 architectures.
comp.unix. programmer	Q&A for people programming under Unix.
comp.unix. questions	UNIX neophytes group.
comp.unix.shell	Using and programming the Unix shell.
comp.unix.sys3	System III UNIX discussions.
comp.unix. sys5.misc	Versions of System V which predate Release 3.
comp.unix.sys5.r3	Discussing System V Release 3.
comp.unix.sys5.r4	Discussing System V Release 4.
comp.unix.ultrix	Discussions about DEC's Ultrix.
comp.unix. unixware	Discussion about Novell's UnixWare products.
comp.unix. user-friendly	Discussion of UNIX user-friendliness.
comp.unix.wizards	For only true Unix wizards.
comp.unix. xenix.misc	General discussions regarding XENIX (except SCO).
comp.unix. xenix.sco	XENIX versions from the Santa Cruz Operation.
comp.virus	Computer viruses & security.

Newsgroup	Description
comp.windows.garnet	The Garnet user interface development environment.
comp.windows.interviews	The InterViews object-oriented windowing system.
comp.windows.misc	Various issues about windowing systems.
comp.windows.news	Sun Microsystems' NeWS window system.
comp.windows.open-look	Discussion about the Open Look GUI.
comp.windows.suit	The SUIT user-interface toolkit.
comp.windows.x	Discussion about the X Window System.
comp.windows.x.announce	X Consortium announcements.
comp.windows.x.apps	Getting and using, not programming, applications for X.
comp.windows.x.i386unix	The XFree86 window system and others.
comp.windows.x.intrinsics	Discussion of the X toolkit.
comp.windows.x.pex	The PHIGS extension of the X Window System.
misc.activism.progressive	Information for Progressive activists.
misc.answers	Repository for periodic USENET articles.
misc.books.technical	Discussion of books about technical topics.
misc.consumers	Consumer interests, product reviews, etc.
misc.consumers.house	Discussion about owning and maintaining a house.

Newsgroup	Description
misc.creativity	Promoting the use of creativity in all human endeavors.
misc.education	Discussion of the educational system.
misc.education. adult	Adult education and adult literacy practice/research.
misc.education. home-school. christian	Christian home-schooling.
misc.education. home-school.misc	Almost anything about home-schooling.
misc.education. language.english	Teaching English to speakers of other languages.
misc.education. medical	Issues related to medical education.
misc.education. multimedia	Multimedia for education.
misc.education. science	Issues related to science education.
misc.emerg-services	Forum for paramedics & other first responders.
misc.entrepreneurs	Discussion on operating a business.
misc.fitness	Physical fitness, exercise, body-building, etc.
misc.forsale	Short, tasteful postings about items for sale.
misc.forsale. computers.d	Discussion of misc.forsale. computers.*.
misc.forsale. computers.mac	Apple Macintosh related computer items.
misc.forsale. computers.other	Selling miscellaneous computer stuff.
misc.forsale. computers.pc-clone	IBM PC related computer items.

Newsgroup	Description
misc.forsale. computers. workstation	Workstation related computer items.
misc.handicap	Items of interest for/about the handicapped.
misc.headlines	Current interest: drug testing, terrorism, etc.
misc.health. alternative	Alternative, complementary, and holistic health care.
misc.health. diabetes	Discussion of diabetes management in day to day life.
misc.int-property	Discussion of intellectual property rights.
misc.invest	Investments and the handling of money.
misc.invest.canada	Investing in Canadian financial markets.
misc.invest.funds	Sharing info about bond, stock, real estate funds.
misc.invest. real-estate	Property investments.
misc.invest.stocks	Forum for sharing info about stocks and options.
misc.invest. technical	Analyzing market trends with technical methods.
misc.jobs.contract	Discussions about contract labor.
misc.jobs.misc	Discussion about employment, workplaces, careers.
misc.jobs.offered	Announcements of positions available.
misc.jobs. offered.entry	Job listings only for entry-level positions.
misc.jobs.resumes	Postings of resumes and "situation wanted" articles.

Newsgroup	Description
misc.kids	Children, their behavior and activities.
misc.kids.computer	The use of computers by children.
misc.kids.vacation	Discussion on all forms of family-oriented vacationing.
misc.legal	Legalities and the ethics of law.
misc.legal.computing	Discussing the legal climate of the computing world.
misc.legal.moderated	All aspects of law.
misc.misc	Various discussions not fitting in any other group.
misc.news.east-europe.rferl	Radio Free Europe/Radio Liberty Daily Report.
misc.news.southasia	News from Bangladesh, India, Nepal, etc.
misc.rural	Devoted to issues concerning rural living.
misc.taxes	Tax laws and advice.
misc.test	For testing of network software.
misc.test.moderated	Testing of posting to moderated groups.
misc.transport.urban-transit	Metropolitan public transportation systems.
misc.wanted	Requests for things that are needed (NOT software).
misc.writing	Discussion of writing in all of its forms.
news.admin.misc	General topics of network news administration.
news.admin.policy	Policy issues of USENET.

Newsgroup	Description
news.admin.technical	Technical aspects of maintaining network news.
news.announce.conferences	Calls for papers and conference announcements.
news.announce.important	General announcements of interest to all.
news.announce.newgroups	Calls for newgroups & announcements of same.
news.announce.newusers	Explanatory postings for new users.
news.answers	Repository for periodic USENET articles.
news.config	Postings of system down times and interruptions.
news.future	The future technology of network news systems.
news.groups	Discussions and lists of newsgroups.
news.groups.questions	Where can I find talk about topic X?
news.groups.reviews	What is going on in group or mailing list named X?
news.lists	News-related statistics and lists.
news.lists.ps-maps	Maps relating to USENET traffic flows.
news.misc	Discussions of USENET itself.
news.newsites	Postings of new site announcements.
news.newusers.questions	Q & A for users new to the Usenet.
news.software.anu-news	VMS B-news software from Australian National Univ.
news.software.b	Discussion about B-news-compatible software.

Newsgroup	Description
news.software.nn	Discussion about the "nn" news reader package.
news.software. notes	Notesfile software from the Univ. of Illinois.
news.software. readers	Discussion of software used to read network news.
Newsgroup	Description.
rec.answers	Repository for periodic USENET articles.
rec.antiques	Discussing antiques and vintage items.
rec.aquaria	Keeping fish and aquaria as a hobby.
rec.arts.animation	Discussion of various kinds of animation.
rec.arts.anime	Japanese animation fen discussion.
rec.arts.anime.info	Announcements about Japanese animation.
rec.arts.anime. marketplace	Things for sale in the Japanese animation world.
rec.arts.anime. stories	All about Japanese comic fanzines.
rec.arts.ascii	ASCII art, info on archives, art, & artists.
rec.arts.bodyart	Tattoos and body decoration discussions.
rec.arts.bonsai	Dwarfish trees and shrubbery.
rec.arts.books	Books of all genres, and the publishing industry.
rec.arts.books. marketplace	Buying and selling of books.
rec.arts.books. tolkien	The works of J.R.R. Tolkien.

Newsgroup	Description
rec.arts.cinema	Discussion of the art of cinema.
rec.arts.comics. creative	Encouraging good superhero-style writing.
rec.arts.comics.info	Reviews, convention information, and other comics news.
rec.arts.comics. marketplace	The exchange of comics and comic related items.
rec.arts.comics.misc	Comic books, graphic novels, sequential art.
rec.arts.comics. strips	Discussion of short-form comics.
rec.arts.comics. xbooks	The Mutant Universe of Marvel Comics.
rec.arts.dance	Any aspects of dance not covered in another newsgroup.
rec.arts.disney	Discussion of any Disney-related subjects.
rec.arts.drwho	Discussion about Dr. Who.
rec.arts.erotica	Erotic fiction and verse.
rec.arts.fine	Fine arts & artists.
rec.arts.int-fiction	Discussions about interactive fiction.
rec.arts.manga	All aspects of the Japanese storytelling art form.
rec.arts.marching. drumcorps	Drum and bugle corps.
rec.arts.marching. misc	Marching-related performance activities.
rec.arts.misc	Discussions about the arts not in other groups.
rec.arts.movies	Discussions of movies and movie making.
rec.arts.movies. production	Filmmaking, amateur and professional.

Newsgroup	Description
rec.arts.movies.reviews	Reviews of movies.
rec.arts.poems	For the posting of poems.
rec.arts.prose	Short works of prose fiction and followup discussion.
rec.arts.sf.announce	Major announcements of the SF world.
rec.arts.sf.fandom	Discussions of SF fan activities.
rec.arts.sf.marketplace	Personal forsale notices of SF materials.
rec.arts.sf.misc	Science fiction lovers' newsgroup.
rec.arts.sf.movies	Discussing SF motion pictures.
rec.arts.sf.reviews	Reviews of science fiction/fantasy/horror works.
rec.arts.sf.science	Real and speculative aspects of SF science.
rec.arts.sf.starwars	Discussion of the Star Wars universe.
rec.arts.sf.tv	Discussing general television SF.
rec.arts.sf.tv.babylon5	Babylon 5 creators meet Babylon 5 fans.
rec.arts.sf.tv.quantum-leap	Quantum Leap TV, comics, cons, etc.
rec.arts.sf.written	Discussion of written science fiction and fantasy.
rec.arts.sf.written.robert-jordan	Books by author Robert Jordan.
rec.arts.startrek.current	New Star Trek shows, movies, and books.
rec.arts.startrek.fandom	Star Trek conventions and memorabilia.

Newsgroup	Description
rec.arts.startrek.info	Information about the universe of Star Trek.
rec.arts.startrek.misc	General discussions of Star Trek.
rec.arts.startrek.reviews	Reviews of Star Trek books, episodes, films, etc.
rec.arts.startrek.tech	Star Trek's depiction of future technologies.
rec.arts.theatre	Discussion of all aspects of stage work & theatre.
rec.arts.theatre.misc	Miscellaneous topics and issues in theatre.
rec.arts.theatre.musicals	Musical theatre around the world.
rec.arts.theatre.plays	Dramaturgy and discussion of plays.
rec.arts.theatre.stagecraft	Issues in stagecraft and production.
rec.arts.tv	The boob tube, its history, and past and current shows.
rec.arts.tv.mst3k	For fans of Mystery Science Theater 3000.
rec.arts.tv.soaps	Postings about soap operas.
rec.arts.tv.uk	Discussions of telly shows from the UK.
rec.arts.wobegon	"A Prairie Home Companion" radio show discussion.
rec.audio	High-fidelity audio.
rec.audio.car	Discussions of automobile audio systems.
rec.audio.high-end	High-end audio systems.
rec.audio.marketplace	Buying and selling of home audio equipment.

Newsgroup	Description
rec.audio.misc	Post about audio here if you can't post anywhere else.
rec.audio.opinion	Everybody's two bits on audio in your home.
rec.audio.pro	Professional audio recording and studio engineering.
rec.audio.tech	Theoretical, factual, and DIY topics in home audio.
rec.autos.antique	Discussing all aspects of automobiles over 25 years old.
rec.autos.driving	Driving automobiles.
rec.autos.marketplace	Buy/Sell/Trade automobiles, parts, tools, accessories.
rec.autos.misc	Miscellaneous discussion about automobiles.
rec.autos.rod-n-custom	High-performance automobiles.
rec.autos.simulators	Discussion of automotive simulators.
rec.autos.sport	Discussion of organized, legal auto competitions.
rec.autos.sport.info	Auto racing news, results, announcements.
rec.autos.sport.nascar	NASCAR and other professional stock car racing.
rec.autos.sport.tech	Technical aspects & technology of auto racing.
rec.autos.tech	Technical aspects of automobiles, et al.
rec.autos.vw	Issues pertaining to Volkswagen products.
rec.aviation.announce	Events of interest to the aviation community.

Newsgroup	Description
rec.aviation.answers	Frequently asked questions about aviation.
rec.aviation.homebuilt	Selecting, designing, building, and restoring aircraft.
rec.aviation.ifr	Flying under Instrument Flight Rules.
rec.aviation.military	Military aircraft of the past, present, and future.
rec.aviation.misc	Miscellaneous topics in aviation.
rec.aviation.owning	Information on owning airplanes.
rec.aviation.piloting	General discussion for aviators.
rec.aviation.products	Reviews and discussion of products useful to pilots.
rec.aviation.questions	Aviation questions and answers.
rec.aviation.simulators	Flight simulation on all levels.
rec.aviation.soaring	All aspects of sailplanes and hang gliders.
rec.aviation.stories	Anecdotes of flight experiences.
rec.aviation.student	Learning to fly.
rec.backcountry	Activities in the Great Outdoors.
rec.bicycles.marketplace	Buying, selling, & reviewing items for cycling.
rec.bicycles.misc	General discussion of bicycling.
rec.bicycles.racing	Bicycle racing techniques, rules, and results.
rec.bicycles.rides	Discussions of tours and training or commuting routes.
rec.bicycles.soc	Societal issues of bicycling.

Newsgroup	Description
rec.bicycles.tech	Cycling product design, construction, maintenance, etc.
rec.birds	Hobbyists interested in bird watching.
rec.boats	Hobbyists interested in boating.
rec.boats.paddle	Talk about any boats with oars, paddles, etc.
rec.climbing	Climbing techniques, competition announcements, etc.
rec.collecting	Discussion among collectors of many things.
rec.collecting.cards	Collecting all sorts of sport and nonsport cards.
rec.collecting.stamps	Discussion of all things related to philately.
rec.crafts.brewing	The art of making beers and meads.
rec.crafts.jewelry	All aspects of jewelry making and lapidary work.
rec.crafts.metalworking	All aspects of working with metal.
rec.crafts.misc	Handiwork arts not covered elsewhere.
rec.crafts.quilting	All about quilts and other quilted items.
rec.crafts.textiles	Sewing, weaving, knitting, and other fiber arts.
rec.crafts.winemaking	The tasteful art of making wine.
rec.equestrian	Discussion of things equestrian.
rec.folk-dancing	Folk dances, dancers, and dancing.
rec.food.cooking	Food, cooking, cookbooks, and recipes.

Newsgroup	Description
rec.food.drink	Wines and spirits.
rec.food.drink.beer	All things beer.
rec.food.drink.coffee	The making and drinking of coffee.
rec.food.historic	The history of food making arts.
rec.food.recipes	Recipes for interesting food and drink.
rec.food.restaurants	Discussion of dining out.
rec.food.sourdough	Making and baking with sourdough.
rec.food.veg	Vegetarians.
rec.food.veg.cooking	Vegetarian recipes, cooking, nutrition.
rec.gambling	Articles on games of chance & betting.
rec.games.abstract	Perfect information, pure strategy games.
rec.games.backgammon	Discussion of the game of backgammon.
rec.games.board	Discussion and hints on board games.
rec.games.board.ce	The Cosmic Encounter board game.
rec.games.board.marketplace	Trading and selling of board games.
rec.games.bolo	The networked strategy war game Bolo.
rec.games.bridge	Hobbyists interested in bridge.
rec.games.chess	Chess & computer chess.
rec.games.chinese-chess	Discussion of the game of Chinese chess, Xiangqi.
rec.games.corewar	The Core War computer challenge.

Newsgroup	Description
rec.games. deckmaster	The Deckmaster line of games.
rec.games. deckmaster. marketplace	Trading of deckmaster paraphernalia.
rec.games.design	Discussion of game design related issues.
rec.games. diplomacy	The conquest game Diplomacy.
rec.games.empire	Discussion and hints about Empire.
rec.games.frp. advocacy	Flames and rebuttals about various role-playing systems.
rec.games.frp. announce	Announcements of happenings in the role-playing world.
rec.games.frp. archives	Archivable fantasy stories and other projects.
rec.games.frp.cyber	Discussions of cyberpunk related roleplaying games.
rec.games.frp.dnd	Fantasy role-playing with TSR's Dungeons and Dragons.
rec.games.frp. live-action	Live-action roleplaying games.
rec.games.frp. marketplace	Role-playing game materials wanted and for sale.
rec.games.frp.misc	General discussions of role-playing games.
rec.games.go	Discussion about Go.
rec.games.hack	Discussion, hints, etc. about the Hack game.
rec.games. int-fiction	All aspects of interactive fiction games.
rec.games.mecha	Giant robot games.

Newsgroup	Description
rec.games.miniatures	Tabletop wargaming.
rec.games.misc	Games and computer games.
rec.games.moria	Comments, hints, and info about the Moria game.
rec.games.mud.admin	Administrative issues of multiuser dungeons.
rec.games.mud.announce	Informational articles about multiuser dungeons.
rec.games.mud.diku	All about DikuMuds.
rec.games.mud.lp	Discussions of the LPMUD computer role playing game.
rec.games.mud.misc	Various aspects of multiuser computer games.
rec.games.mud.tiny	Discussion about Tiny muds, like MUSH, MUSE, and MOO.
rec.games.netrek	Discussion of the X window system game Netrek (XtrekII).
rec.games.pbm	Discussion about Play by Mail games.
rec.games.pinball	Discussing pinball-related issues.
rec.games.programmer	Discussion of adventure game programming.
rec.games.rogue	Discussion and hints about Rogue.
rec.games.roguelike.angband	The computer game Angband.
rec.games.roguelike.announce	Major info about rogue-style games.
rec.games.roguelike.misc	Rogue-style dungeon games without other groups.
rec.games.roguelike.moria	The computer game Moria.

Newsgroup	Description
rec.games.roguelike.nethack	The computer game Nethack.
rec.games.roguelike.rogue	The computer game Rogue.
rec.games.trivia	Discussion about trivia.
rec.games.video.3do	Discussion of 3DO video game systems.
rec.games.video.advocacy	Debate on merits of various video game systems.
rec.games.video.arcade	Discussions about coin-operated video games.
rec.games.video.arcade.collecting	Collecting, converting, repairing etc.
rec.games.video.atari	Discussion of Atari's video game systems.
rec.games.video.cd32	Gaming talk, info, and help for the Amiga CD32.
rec.games.video.classic	Older home video entertainment systems.
rec.games.video.marketplace	Home video game stuff for sale or trade.
rec.games.video.misc	General discussion about home video games.
rec.games.video.nintendo	All Nintendo video game systems and software.
rec.games.video.sega	All Sega video game systems and software.
rec.games.xtank.play	Strategy and tactics for the distributed game Xtank.
rec.games.xtank.programmer	Coding the Xtank game and its robots.
rec.gardens	Gardening, methods and results.
rec.gardens.orchids	Growing, hybridizing, and general care of orchids.

Newsgroup	Description
rec.gardens.roses	Gardening information related to roses.
rec.guns	Discussions about firearms.
rec.heraldry	Discussion of coats of arms.
rec.humor	Jokes and the like. May be somewhat offensive.
rec.humor.d	Discussions on the content of rec.humor articles.
rec.humor.funny	Jokes that are funny (in the moderator's opinion).
rec.humor.oracle	Sagacious advice from the USENET Oracle.
rec.humor.oracle.d	Comments about the USENET Oracle's comments.
rec.hunting	Discussions about hunting.
rec.juggling	Juggling techniques, equipment and events.
rec.kites	Talk about kites and kiting.
rec.mag	Magazine summaries, tables of contents, etc.
rec.martial-arts	Discussion of the various martial art forms.
rec.misc	General topics about recreational/participant sports.
rec.models.railroad	Model railroads of all scales.
rec.models.rc	Radio-controlled models for hobbyists.
rec.models.rockets	Model rockets for hobbyists.
rec.models.scale	Construction of models.
rec.motorcycles	Motorcycles and related products and laws.
rec.motorcycles. dirt	Riding motorcycles and ATVs off-road.

Newsgroup	Description
rec.motorcycles.harley	All aspects of Harley-Davidson motorcycles.
rec.motorcycles.racing	Discussion of all aspects of racing motorcycles.
rec.music.a-cappella	Vocal music without instrumental accompaniment.
rec.music.afro-latin	Music with Afro-Latin, African, and Latin influences.
rec.music.beatles	Postings about the Fab Four & their music.
rec.music.bluenote	Discussion of jazz, blues, and related types of music.
rec.music.cd	CDs: availability and other discussions.
rec.music.celtic	Traditional and modern music with a Celtic flavor.
rec.music.christian	Christian music, both contemporary and traditional.
rec.music.classical	Discussion about classical music.
rec.music.classical.guitar	Classical music performed on guitar.
rec.music.classical.performing	Performing classical (including early) music.
rec.music.compose	Creating musical and lyrical works.
rec.music.country.western	C&W music, performers, performances, etc.
rec.music.dementia	Discussion of comedy and novelty music.
rec.music.dylan	Discussion of Bob's works & music.
rec.music.early	Discussion of preclassical European music.

Newsgroup	Description
rec.music.folk	Folks discussing folk music of various sorts.
rec.music.funky	Funk, rap, hip-hop, house, soul, r&b, and related.
rec.music.gaffa	Discussion of Kate Bush & other alternative music.
rec.music.gdead	A group for (Grateful) Dead-heads.
rec.music.indian. classical	Hindustani and Carnatic Indian classical music.
rec.music. indian.misc	Discussing Indian music in general.
rec.music.industrial	Discussion of all industrial-related music styles.
rec.music.info	News and announcements on musical topics.
rec.music.makers	For performers and their discussions.
rec.music. makers.bass	Upright bass and bass guitar techniques and equipment.
rec.music. makers.builders	Design, building, repair of musical instruments.
rec.music. makers.guitar	Electric and acoustic guitar techniques and equipment.
rec.music.makers. guitar.acoustic	Discussion of acoustic guitar playing.
rec.music.makers. guitar.tablature	Guitar tablature/chords.
rec.music.makers. marketplace	Buying & selling used music-making equipment.
rec.music.makers. percussion	Drum & other percussion techniques & equipment.
rec.music. makers.piano	Piano music, performing, composing, learning, styles.

Newsgroup	Description
rec.music.makers.synth	Synthesizers and computer music.
rec.music.marketplace	Records, tapes, and CDs: wanted, for sale, etc.
rec.music.misc	Music lovers' group.
rec.music.movies	Music for movies and television.
rec.music.newage	"New Age" music discussions.
rec.music.phish	Discussing the musical group Phish.
rec.music.reggae	Roots, Rockers, Dancehall Reggae.
rec.music.rem	The musical group R.E.M.
rec.music.reviews	Reviews of music of all genres and mediums.
rec.music.video	Discussion of music videos and music video software.
rec.nude	Hobbyists interested in naturist/nudist activities.
rec.org.mensa	Talking with members of the high IQ society Mensa.
rec.org.sca	Society for Creative Anachronism.
rec.outdoors.fishing	All aspects of sport and commercial fishing.
rec.outdoors.fishing.fly	Fly fishing in general.
rec.outdoors.fishing.saltwater	Saltwater fishing, methods, gear, Q&A.
rec.parks.theme	Entertainment theme parks.
rec.pets	Pets, pet care, and household animals in general.
rec.pets.birds	The culture and care of indoor birds.

Newsgroup	Description
rec.pets.cats	Discussion about domestic cats.
rec.pets.dogs	Any and all subjects relating to dogs as pets.
rec.pets.herp	Reptiles, amphibians, and other exotic vivarium pets.
rec.photo	Hobbyists interested in photography.
rec.photo.advanced	Advanced topics (equipment and technique).
rec.photo.darkroom	Developing, printing, and other darkroom issues.
rec.photo.help	Beginners' questions about photography (and answers).
rec.photo.marketplace	Trading of personal photographic equipment.
rec.photo.misc	General issues related to photography.
rec.puzzles	Puzzles, problems, and quizzes.
rec.puzzles.crosswords	Making and playing gridded word puzzles.
rec.pyrotechnics	Fireworks, rocketry, safety, & other topics.
rec.radio.amateur.antenna	Antennas: theory, techniques, and construction.
rec.radio.amateur.digital.misc	Packet radio and other digital radio modes.
rec.radio.amateur.equipment	All about production amateur radio hardware.
rec.radio.amateur.homebrew	Amateur radio construction and experimentation.
rec.radio.amateur.misc	Amateur radio practices, contests, events, rules, etc.
rec.radio.amateur.policy	Radio use & regulation policy.

Newsgroup	Description
rec.radio.amateur. space	Amateur radio transmissions through space.
rec.radio .broadcasting	Discussion of global domestic broadcast radio.
rec.radio.cb	Citizen-band radio.
rec.radio.info	Informational postings related to radio.
rec.radio.noncomm	Topics relating to noncommercial radio.
rec.radio.scanner	"Utility" broadcasting traffic above 30 MHz.
rec.radio.shortwave	Shortwave radio enthusiasts.
rec.radio.swap	Offers to trade and swap radio equipment.
rec.railroad	For fans of real trains, ferroequinologists.
rec.roller-coaster	Roller coasters and other amusement park rides.
rec.running	Running for enjoyment, sport, exercise, etc.
rec.scouting	Scouting youth organizations worldwide.
rec.scuba	Hobbyists interested in SCUBA diving.
rec.skate	Ice skating and roller skating.
rec.skiing.alpine	Downhill skiing technique, equipment, etc.
rec.skiing. announce	FAQ, competition results, automated snow reports.
rec.skiing.nordic	Cross-country skiing technique, equipment, etc.
rec.skiing. snowboard	Snowboarding technique, equipment, etc.

Newsgroup	Description
rec.skydiving	Hobbyists interested in skydiving.
rec.sport.baseball	Discussion about baseball.
rec.sport.baseball.analysis	Analysis & discussion of baseball.
rec.sport.baseball.college	Baseball on the collegiate level.
rec.sport.baseball.data	Raw baseball data (stats, birthdays, scheds.).
rec.sport.baseball.fantasy	Rotisserie (fantasy) baseball play.
rec.sport.basketball.college	Hoops on the collegiate level.
rec.sport.basketball.misc	Discussion about basketball.
rec.sport.basketball.pro	Talk of professional basketball.
rec.sport.basketball.women	Women's basketball at all levels.
rec.sport.boxing	Boxing in all its pugilistic facets and forms.
rec.sport.cricket	Discussion about the sport of cricket.
rec.sport.cricket.info	News, scores, and info related to cricket.
rec.sport.disc	Discussion of flying disc based sports.
rec.sport.fencing	All aspects of swordplay.
rec.sport.football.australian	Discussion of Australian (Rules) Football.
rec.sport.football.canadian	All about Canadian rules football.
rec.sport.football.college	US-style college football.

Newsgroup	Description
rec.sport.football.fantasy	Rotisserie (fantasy) football play.
rec.sport.football.misc	Discussion about American-style football.
rec.sport.football.pro	US-style professional football.
rec.sport.golf	Discussion about all aspects of golfing.
rec.sport.hockey	Discussion about ice hockey.
rec.sport.hockey.field	Discussion of the sport of field hockey.
rec.sport.misc	Spectator sports.
rec.sport.olympics	All aspects of the Olympic Games.
rec.sport.paintball	Discussing all aspects of the survival game paintball.
rec.sport.pro-wrestling	Discussion about professional wrestling.
rec.sport.rowing	Crew for competition or fitness.
rec.sport.rugby	Discussion about the game of rugby.
rec.sport.soccer	Discussion about soccer (Association Football).
rec.sport.swimming	Training for and competing in swimming events.
rec.sport.table-tennis	Things related to table tennis (aka Ping Pong).
rec.sport.tennis	Things related to the sport of tennis.
rec.sport.triathlon	Discussing all aspects of multi-event sports.
rec.sport.volleyball	Discussion about volleyball.
rec.sport.water-polo	Discussion of water polo.

Newsgroup	Description
rec.sport.waterski	Waterskiing and other boat-towed activities.
rec.toys.lego	Discussion of Lego, Duplo (and compatible) toys.
rec.toys.misc	Discussion of toys that lack a specific newsgroup.
rec.travel	Traveling all over the world.
rec.travel.air	Airline travel around the world.
rec.travel.asia	Travel in Asia.
rec.travel.cruises	Travel by cruise ship.
rec.travel.europe	Travel in Europe.
rec.travel.marketplace	Tickets and accomodations wanted and for sale.
rec.travel.misc	Everything and anything about travel.
rec.travel.usa-canada	Travel in the United States and Canada.
rec.video	Video and video components.
rec.video.cable-tv	Technical and regulatory issues of cable television.
rec.video.desktop	Amateur, computer-based video editing and production.
rec.video.production	Making professional-quality video productions.
rec.video.releases	Prerecorded video releases on laserdisc and videotape.
rec.video.satellite	Getting shows via satellite.
rec.windsurfing	Riding the waves as a hobby.
rec.woodworking	Hobbyists interested in woodworking.
sci.aeronautics	The science of aeronautics & related technology.

Newsgroup	Description
sci.aeronautics.airliners	Airliner technology.
sci.aeronautics.simulation	Aerospace simulation technology.
sci.agriculture	Farming, agriculture, and related topics.
sci.agriculture.beekeeping	Beekeeping, bee-culture, and hive products.
sci.answers	Repository for periodic USENET articles.
sci.anthropology	All aspects of studying human-kind.
sci.anthropology.paleo	Evolution of man and other primates.
sci.aquaria	Only scientifically oriented postings about aquaria.
sci.archaeology	Studying antiquities of the world.
sci.archaeology.mesoamerican	The field of mesoamerican archaeology.
sci.astro	Astronomy discussions and information.
sci.astro.fits	Issues related to the Flexible Image Transport System.
sci.astro.hubble	Processing Hubble Space Telescope data.
sci.astro.planetarium	Discussion of planetariums.
sci.astro.research	Forum in astronomy/astrophysics research.
sci.bio	Biology and related sciences.
sci.bio.ecology	Ecological research.
sci.bio.ethology	Animal behavior and behavioral ecology.

Newsgroup	Description
sci.bio.evolution	Discussions of evolutionary biology.
sci.bio.herp	Biology of amphibians and reptiles.
sci.chem	Chemistry and related sciences.
sci.chem.electrochem	The field of electrochemistry.
sci.chem.labware	Chemical laboratory equipment.
sci.chem.organomet	Organometallic chemistry.
sci.classics	Studying classical history, languages, art, and more.
sci.cognitive	Perception, memory, judgement, and reasoning.
sci.comp-aided	The use of computers as tools in scientific research.
sci.cryonics	Theory and practice of biostasis, suspended animation.
sci.crypt	Different methods of data en/decryption.
sci.data.formats	Modelling, storage, and retrieval of scientific data.
sci.econ	The science of economics.
sci.econ.research	Research in all fields of economics.
sci.edu	The science of education.
sci.electronics	Circuits, theory, electrons, and discussions.
sci.electronics.cad	Schematic drafting, printed circuit layout, simulation.
sci.electronics.repair	Fixing electronic equipment.
sci.energy	Discussions about energy, science, & technology.

Newsgroup	Description
sci.energy.hydrogen	All about hydrogen as an alternative fuel.
sci.engr	Technical discussions about engineering tasks.
sci.engr.advanced-tv	HDTV/DATV standards, formats, equipment, practices.
sci.engr.biomed	Discussing the field of biomedical engineering.
sci.engr.chem	All aspects of chemical engineering.
sci.engr.civil	Topics related to civil engineering.
sci.engr.control	The engineering of control systems.
sci.engr.lighting	Light, vision, & color in architecture, media, etc.
sci.engr.manufacturing	Manufacturing technology.
sci.engr.mech	The field of mechanical engineering.
sci.engr.semiconductors	Semiconductor devices, processes, materials, physics.
sci.environment	Discussions about the environment and ecology.
sci.fractals	Objects of nonintegral dimension and other chaos.
sci.geo.eos	NASA's Earth Observation System (EOS).
sci.geo.fluids	Discussion of geophysical fluid dynamics.
sci.geo.geology	Discussion of solid earth sciences.
sci.geo.hydrology	Surface and groundwater hydrology.

Newsgroup	Description
sci.geo.meteorology	Discussion of meteorology and related topics.
sci.geo.satellite-nav	Satellite navigation systems, especially GPS.
sci.image.processing	Scientific image processing and analysis.
sci.lang	Natural languages, communication, etc.
sci.lang.japan	The Japanese language, both spoken and written.
sci.life-extension	Slowing, stopping, or reversing the ageing process.
sci.logic	Logic: math, philosophy, & computational aspects.
sci.materials	All aspects of materials engineering.
sci.math	Mathematical discussions and pursuits.
sci.math.research	Discussion of current mathematical research.
sci.math.symbolic	Symbolic algebra discussion.
sci.mech.fluids	All aspects of fluid mechanics.
sci.med	Medicine and its related products and regulations.
sci.med.aids	AIDS: treatment, pathology/biology of HIV, prevention.
sci.med.dentistry	Dentally related topics; all about teeth.
sci.med.nursing	Nursing questions and discussion.
sci.med.nutrition	Physiological impacts of diet.
sci.med.occupational	Preventing, detecting, & treating occupational injuries.

Newsgroup	Description
sci.med.pharmacy	The teaching and practice of pharmacy.
sci.med.physics	Issues of physics in medical testing/care.
sci.med.psychobiology	Dialog and news in psychiatry and psychobiology.
sci.med.radiology	All aspects of radiology.
sci.med.telemedicine	Hospital/physician networks. No diagnosis questions.
sci.military	Discussion about science & the military.
sci.misc	Short-lived discussions on subjects in the sciences.
sci.nanotech	Self-reproducing molecular-scale machines.
sci.nonlinear	Chaotic systems and other nonlinear scientific study.
sci.op-research	Research, teaching, & application of operations research.
sci.optics	Discussion relating to the science of optics.
sci.philosophy.tech	Technical philosophy: math, science, logic, etc.
sci.physics	Physical laws, properties, etc.
sci.physics.accelerators	Particle accelerators and the physics of beams.
sci.physics.computational.fluid-dynamics	Computaional fluid dynamics.
sci.physics.electromag	Electromagnetic theory and applications.
sci.physics.fusion	Info on fusion, esp. "cold" fusion.
sci.physics.particle	Particle physics discussions.

Newsgroup	Description
sci.physics.plasma	Plasma Science & Technology community exchange.
sci.physics.research	Current physics research.
sci.polymers	All aspects of polymer science.
sci.psychology	Topics related to psychology.
sci.psychology. digest	PSYCOLOQUY: Refereed Psychology Journal and Newsletter.
sci.psychology. research	Research issues in psychology.
sci.research	Research methods, funding, ethics, and whatever.
sci.research.careers	Issues relevant to careers in scientific research.
sci.research.postdoc	Anything about postdoctoral studies, including offers.
sci.skeptic	Skeptics discussing pseudo-science.
sci.space.news	Announcements of space-related news items.
sci.space.policy	Discussions about space policy.
sci.space.science	Space and planetary science and related technical work.
sci.space.shuttle	The space shuttle and the STS program.
sci.space.tech	Technical and general issues related to space flight.
sci.stat.consult	Statistical consulting.
sci.stat.edu	Statistics education.
sci.stat.math	Statistics from a strictly mathematical viewpoint.
sci.systems	The theory and application of systems science.

Newsgroup	Description
sci.techniques.mag-resonance	Magnetic resonance imaging and spectroscopy.
sci.techniques.microscopy	The field of microscopy.
sci.techniques.spectroscopy	Spectrum analysis.
sci.techniques.xtallography	The field of crystallography.
sci.virtual-worlds	Virtual Reality: technology and culture.
sci.virtual-worlds.apps	Current and future uses of virtual-worlds technology.
soc.answers	Repository for periodic USENET articles.
soc.bi	Discussions of bisexuality.
soc.college	College, college activities, campus life, etc.
soc.college.grad	General issues related to graduate schools.
soc.college.gradinfo	Information about graduate schools.
soc.college.org.aiesec	The Int'l Assoc. of Business and Commerce Students.
soc.college.teaching-asst	Issues affecting collegiate teaching assistants.
soc.couples	Discussions for couples (cf. soc.singles).
soc.couples.intercultural	Inter-cultural and inter-racial relationships.
soc.culture.afghanistan	Discussion of the Afghan society.
soc.culture.african	Discussions about Africa & things African.

Newsgroup	Description
soc.culture.african.american	Discussions about Afro-American issues.
soc.culture.arabic	Technological & cultural issues, *not* politics.
soc.culture.argentina	All about life in Argentina.
soc.culture.asean	Countries of the Assoc. of SE Asian Nations.
soc.culture.asian.american	Issues & discussion about Asian-Americans.
soc.culture.australian	Australian culture and society.
soc.culture.austria	Austria and its people.
soc.culture.baltics	People of the Baltic states.
soc.culture.bangladesh	Issues & discussion about Bangladesh.
soc.culture.belgium	Belgian society, culture(s), and people.
soc.culture.berber	The berber language, history, and culture.
soc.culture.bosna-herzgvna	The independent state of Bosnia and Herzegovina.
soc.culture.brazil	Talking about the people and country of Brazil.
soc.culture.british	Issues about Britain & those of British descent.
soc.culture.bulgaria	Discussing Bulgarian society.
soc.culture.burma	Politics, culture, news, discussion about Burma.
soc.culture.canada	Discussions of Canada and its people.
soc.culture.caribbean	Life in the Caribbean.

Newsgroup	Description
soc.culture.celtic	Irish, Scottish, Breton, Cornish, Manx, & Welsh.
soc.culture.chile	All about Chile and its people.
soc.culture.china	About China and Chinese culture.
soc.culture. colombia	Colombian talk, social, politics, science.
soc.culture.croatia	The lives of people of Croatia.
soc.culture.cuba	Cuban culture, society, and politics.
soc.culture. czecho-slovak	Bohemian, Slovak, Moravian, and Silesian life.
soc.culture.europe	Discussing all aspects of all-European society.
soc.culture.filipino	Group about the Filipino culture.
soc.culture.french	French culture, history, and related discussions.
soc.culture.german	Discussions about German culture and history.
soc.culture.greek	Group about Greeks.
soc.culture. hongkong	Discussions pertaining to Hong Kong.
soc.culture. hongkong. entertainment	Entertainment in Hong Kong.
soc.culture.indian	Group for discussion about India & things Indian.
soc.culture. indian.info	Info group for soc.culture.indian, etc.
soc.culture.indian. telugu	The culture of the Telugu people of India.
soc.culture. indonesia	All about the Indonesian nation.

Newsgroup	Description
soc.culture.iranian	Discussions about Iran and things Iranian/Persian.
soc.culture.israel	Israel and Israelis.
soc.culture.italian	The Italian people and their culture.
soc.culture.japan	Everything Japanese, except the Japanese language.
soc.culture.jewish	Jewish culture & religion. (cf. talk.politics.mideast)
soc.culture.jewish.holocaust	The Shoah.
soc.culture.korean	Discussions about Korea & things Korean.
soc.culture.laos	Cultural and Social Aspects of Laos.
soc.culture.latin-america	Topics about Latin-America.
soc.culture.lebanon	Discussion about things Lebanese.
soc.culture.maghreb	North African society and culture.
soc.culture.magyar	The Hungarian people & their culture.
soc.culture.malaysia	All about Malaysian society.
soc.culture.mexican	Discussion of Mexico's society.
soc.culture.mexican.american	Mexican-American/Chicano culture and issues.
soc.culture.misc	Group for discussion about other cultures.
soc.culture.mongolian	Everything related to Mongols and Mongolia.

Newsgroup	Description
soc.culture.native	Aboriginal people around the world.
soc.culture.nepal	Discussion of people and things in & from Nepal.
soc.culture.netherlands	People from the Netherlands and Belgium.
soc.culture.new-zealand	Discussion of topics related to New Zealand.
soc.culture.nordic	Discussion about culture, up north.
soc.culture.pakistan	Topics of discussion about Pakistan.
soc.culture.palestine	Palestinian people, culture, and politics.
soc.culture.peru	All about the people of Peru.
soc.culture.polish	Polish culture, Polish past, and Polish politics.
soc.culture.portuguese	Discussion of the people of Portugal.
soc.culture.puerto-rico	Puerto Rican culture, society, and politics.
soc.culture.romanian	Discussion of Romanian and Moldavian people.
soc.culture.scientists	Cultural issues about scientists & scientific projects.
soc.culture.singapore	The past, present, and future of Singapore.
soc.culture.slovenia	Slovenia and Slovenian people.
soc.culture.somalia	Somalian affairs, society, and culture.
soc.culture.soviet	Topics relating to Russian or Soviet culture.
soc.culture.spain	Spain and the Spanish.

Newsgroup	Description
soc.culture.sri-lanka	Things & people from Sri Lanka.
soc.culture.swiss	Swiss culture.
soc.culture.taiwan	Discussion about things Taiwanese.
soc.culture.tamil	Tamil language, history, and culture.
soc.culture.thai	Thai people and their culture.
soc.culture.turkish	Discussion about things Turkish.
soc.culture.ukrainian	The lives and times of the Ukrainian people.
soc.culture.uruguay	Discussions of Uruguay for those at home and abroad.
soc.culture.usa	The culture of the United States of America.
soc.culture.venezuela	Discussion of topics related to Venezuela.
soc.culture.vietnamese	Issues and discussions of Vietnamese culture.
soc.culture.yugoslavia	Discussions of Yugoslavia and its people.
soc.feminism	Discussion of feminism & feminist issues.
soc.history	Discussions of things historical.
soc.history.moderated	All aspects of history.
soc.history.war.misc	History & events of wars in general.
soc.history.war.world-war-ii	History & events of World War Two.
soc.libraries.talk	Discussing all aspects of libraries.
soc.men	Issues related to men, their problems & relationships.

Newsgroup	Description
soc.misc	Socially oriented topics not in other groups.
soc.motss	Issues pertaining to homosexuality.
soc.net-people	Announcements, requests, etc. about people on the net.
soc.org.nonprofit	Nonprofit organizations.
soc.org.service-clubs.misc	General info on all service topics.
soc.penpals	In search of net.friendships.
soc.politics	Political problems, systems, solutions.
soc.politics.arms-d	Arms discussion digest.
soc.religion.bahai	Discussion of the Baha'i Faith.
soc.religion.christian	Christianity and related topics.
soc.religion.christian.bible-study	Examining the Holy Bible.
soc.religion.christian.youth-work	Christians working with young people.
soc.religion.eastern	Discussions of Eastern religions.
soc.religion.gnosis	Gnosis, marifat, jnana, & direct sacred experience.
soc.religion.islam	Discussions of the Islamic faith.
soc.religion.quaker	The Religious Society of Friends.
soc.religion.shamanism	Discussion of the full range of shamanic experience.
soc.rights.human	Human rights & activism (e.g., Amnesty International).
soc.roots	Discussing genealogy and genealogical matters.

Newsgroup	Description
soc.singles	Newsgroup for single people, their activities, etc.
soc.support.transgendered	Transgendered and intersexed persons.
soc.veterans	Social issues relating to military veterans.
soc.women	Issues related to women, their problems & relationships.
talk.abortion	All sorts of discussions and arguments on abortion.
talk.answers	Repository for periodic USENET articles.
talk.bizarre	The unusual, bizarre, curious, and often stupid.
talk.environment	Discussion of the state of the environment & what to do.
talk.origins	Evolution versus creationism (sometimes hot!).
talk.philosophy.misc	Philosophical musings on all topics.
talk.politics.animals	The use and/or abuse of animals.
talk.politics.china	Discussion of political issues related to China.
talk.politics.crypto	The relation between cryptography and government.
talk.politics.drugs	The politics of drug issues.
talk.politics.guns	The politics of firearm ownership and (mis)use.
talk.politics.medicine	The politics and ethics involved with health care.
talk.politics.mideast	Discussion & debate over Middle Eastern events.
talk.politics.misc	Political discussions and ravings of all kinds.

Newsgroup	Description
talk.politics.soviet	Discussion of Soviet politics, domestic and foreign.
talk.politics.theory	Theory of politics and political systems.
talk.politics.tibet	The politics of Tibet and the Tibetan people.
talk.rape	Discussions on stopping rape; not to be crossposted.
talk.religion.misc	Religious, ethical, & moral implications.
talk.religion.newage	Esoteric and minority religions & philosophies.
talk.rumors	For the posting of rumors.

Glossary

alias Something your local Mafia member has. Actually a way to create an alternate name for a command or list as a typing shortcut.

article A message located in an Internet newsgroup.

ASCII Pronounced "ASK-ee." A standard definition of how to represent text characters in a computer so that all computers can understand them. Only represents letters in the American alphabet.

backbone Connected to the neckbone. Really a mechanism through which several networks connect.

baud rate How quickly a modem sends or receives data. The bigger the number, the faster the transfer.

BBS Acronym for Bulletin Board System.

binary file A computer readable file that is not readable by humans. Usually contains a program that you can run, but can contain sounds, video, or pictures.

bulletin board system A computer version of the cork bulletin board. Other computers can connect, usually via modem, to leave messages or files and read those left by others.

chat The computer equivalent of a telephone party line. The chat system divides into groups or channels where everyone connected "talks" at once. As you type, everyone connected to the channel sees what you type.

compressed files Files that have been shrunk in size by a compression program but still maintain all the information intact. Used to save space on disks and to reduce transfer time. Must be uncompressed to be useful again. Examples of compression programs are PKZip, StuffIt, and tar.

cyberpunk A veteran navigator of cyberspace, with an attitude.

cyberspace The virtual area made up by the services of the Internet. While not a physical place, you can accomplish many things you can accomplish in "the real world."

dedicated line   A telephone line that goes above and beyond the call of duty. Actually a leased line from the telephone company, usually high speed, that is kept open all the time and used only for network connections.

dial-in service   For those of us with no budget for a dedicated line. You connect to this service via telephone and modem. Once connected, your computer acts as if it is a terminal connected to your service provider's computer.

dial-in direct connection   A way to fake being on a dedicated line via a modem. With a protocol, such as SLIP or PPP, your modem pretends that your computer is directly connected to the Internet, so you can use various client programs, such as Mosaic or Gopher, directly from your computer.

Domain Name System   A naming convention that defines the address of a computer on the Internet in terms understandable by a mere human. The DNS translates English names into IP addresses. For example, the name world.std.com translates to the IP address 192.203.74.1. See *IP addresses*.

download   The process of transferring information from another computer to yours. You can use this term when referring to files or to other information. See *upload*.

electronic mail   A way for people to send messages back and forth via computer network. Anyone with an address on the Internet can send mail messages to each other. Maybe this will bring back letter writing as a communication vehicle between people.

e-mail   Short for electronic mail.

emoticon   A little picture made out of characters to indicate a particular emotion when looked at sideways. For example, :-) indicates a grin. Used often in e-mail and newsgroup postings to show an emotion that isn't obvious from the text, such as sarcasm. See *smiley*.

encryption　A way to store data so that unauthorized people cannot read it without knowing the password.

Ethernet　A hardware system that you can use to connect computers to each other in a network.

FAQ　Lists of Frequently-Asked-Questions about a topic, usually stored in text files someplace on the Internet. If you are new to an area on the Internet, try to find the FAQ first.

Fidonet　A network connected to the Internet.

file transfer　Copying files from one computer to another, whether by network or by modem.

flame　A nasty message either posted to a newsgroup or sent as e-mail, usually in response to something someone else has written. Don't flame; it's unattractive.

forum　The CompuServe and America Online term for their equivalents to newsgroups. See *newsgroup*.

freeware　Software that you can use for free. The original author usually retains the copyright. Many good programs are free, but often you get what you pay for. See *shareware*.

FTP　File Transfer Protocol. A protocol for two computers to use when transferring files back and forth. Also, in lowercase, the name of a program (ftp) that will let you transfer files using this protocol.

FTP site　A server on the Internet that contains files that you can download using ftp.

gateway　A system that connects two normally incompatible computers together. The computer equivalent of a simultaneous translator at the United Nations.

Gopher　A system to provide a menu-driven access to various resources on the Internet.

GUI　Graphical user interface, pronounced "GOO-ee." An interface to tell a program what to do that uses icons, menus, and the mouse in a pictorial way, rather than commands typed at a keyboard.

host A computer connected to the Internet that lets other computers connect to it.

HTML HyperText Markup Language. A page description language that lets you layout pages that are readable by browsers on the World Wide Web. Describes things such as which text is bold and what links are available, and so on.

HTTP HyperText Transfer Protocol. The mechanism that the World Wide Web uses to link HTML documents to each other across computers on the Net.

Hypermedia Hypertext, but with the addition of other media beyond text, such as pictures, video, and sounds.

Hypertext Text that contains links to other topics, such as an encyclopedia. Clicking on text that contains a link (usually underlined or colored) automatically takes you to the topic referred to by the text.

Internet Protocol The basic communications mechanism that computers on the Internet use to send packets of information to each other.

IP address A numeric address that is unique for each computer on the Internet. They are four-byte numbers, where each byte is separated by a period. For example, 192.203.74.1. Very easy to remember. See *Domain Name System*.

Kermit A public-domain file transfer mechanism that lets computers send files over a modem. See *XMODEM, ZMODEM*.

LISTSERV lists An electronic mailing list that automatically reflects any messages sent to it to all members of the list.

logging on The procedure you use to ask for authorization to connect to a computer and use its services. Usually this involves having a unique user name and password.

logging off Saying bye-bye to the computer you have logged onto.

mail gateway   A system that transfers e-mail messages from two different computer systems.

megabyte   One million bytes (actually 1,048,576 bytes, but who's counting). Used as a measurement of data size and storage capabilities of pieces of a computer system. A megabyte is a lot of typing.

modem   It's what you use to hook your computer via the phone to another one. A modem converts digital information from your computer into tones to be sent over the phone line to another computer and then converts the tones that it receives back into digital information to go into your computer.

MUD   An interactive, multi-user text-based game, such as Zork or Adventure. Stands for Multiple User Dungeons or Dimensions. Every person playing has a character who can wander around the MUD killing monsters, talking to other players, and accumulating wealth and power. Can be confusing to start playing. If you want a way to kill lots of time, this is it.

netiquette   The rules of acceptable behavior on the Internet. How not to be rude on the Internet. Simply, don't waste resources and be nice to people on the other end of the computer line.

Netnews   Alternate name for the USENET newsgroups.

newsgroup   Has nothing to do with news in the traditional sense. The Internet version of a discussion group where people can leave messages for each other on particular topic areas and respond to messages posted by others. See *BBS*.

newsreader   A program that lets you browse messages in various newsgroups and respond to them.

node   Any device that connects to a computer network. It may be another computer or something such as a printer or fax machine.

ping   A simple program that tests a connection between two computers. It just sends one message and waits for a response back.

Point-to-Point Protocol (PPP) a method by which a computer connected by a modem can look like a directly connected Internet host. See *dial-in direct connection*.

port A particular channel that you plug in to transmit data. On your computer, that may be the plug in the back to which you connect your modem. On the Internet, these plugs may be software channels. For example, you can telnet to a particular port on a host. This allows the host to manage multiple channels at once.

protocol A code of behavior that tells different computers how to communicate with each other. Effectively, a simplistic language that each computer agrees to speak and adhere to during communications.

public domain software Software that has no copyrights that you can use and modify without payment.

remote login A way to have your computer log on to another computer in such a way that anything you do on your computer's keyboard acts as if your keyboard is actually connected to the other computer.

rot13 An encryption scheme used in newsgroups to prevent inadvertent reading of offensive messages. You need to decrypt the message before you can read it.

Serial Line Internet Protocol (SLIP) A method by which a computer connected by a modem can look like a directly connected Internet host. See *dial-in direct connection*.

server A computer system that provides services to a client computer. For example, Archie servers actually contain and send back data to clients who request it.

service provider Someone who provides you with a connection to the Internet, whether via dial-up or direct connection.

SGML Standard Generalized Markup Language. A nonproprietary page description language that defines how a page is laid out. Useful for translating documents between word processors or desktop publishing software.

shareware   A method of distributing software where you get it for free, but if you like it and continue to use it, you should pay the author a small fee. Payment is by word of honor, but you usually get some bonus for paying (such as the key that unlocks special features).

shell   In UNIX, a program that accepts your typed commands and tells the operating system what to do. Unlike DOS, there is no single set of commands. UNIX depends on the shell you are using, although most shells share a common set of commands to avoid too much confusion.

signature   A small amount of text that you append to your e-mail messages and postings to newsgroups. Usually contain alternative ways for someone to get in touch with you besides e-mail, such as your phone, fax, and snail-mail address. Sometimes people use cute sayings.

smiley   The nontechnical term for an emoticon.

TCP/IP   Transmission Control Protocol/Internet Protocol. An extension of the Internet Protocol that specifies another aspect of how computers communicate with each other.

Telnet   A program that lets you do a remote login to another computer. See *remote login*.

upload   The process of transferring information from your computer to another. You can use this term when referring to files or to other information. See *download*.

URL   Uniform Resource Locators. Specification that uniquely identifies where you can find a resource in the World Wide Web.

USENET   The "User's Network," a large network connected to the Internet. This network is responsible for distributing and maintaining the 10,000+ newsgroups.

uudecode   The reverse process of uuencode. (Duh!) Translates a uuencoded ASCII file back into a binary file.

uuencode   A program used to convert a binary file into an ASCII file so that it can be transmitted as a text message.

VT100   A computer terminal manufactured by Digital Equipment Corporation in the '70s. The way programs wrote to these screens has become a de facto standard that is duplicated by many other terminals and terminal programs.

W3   Shorthand for the World Wide Web.

World Wide Web   A hypertext system that links documents together so you can navigate by clicking on topics that interest you. The Web is distributed so documents can exist on any computer on the Internet without your having to know where they reside. The coolest new thing on the Net.

XMODEM   A transfer protocol that defines how computers can send files to each other. Not as sophisticated as ZMODEM.

ZIP file   A file that contains files that have been compressed by the program PKZIP under DOS.

ZMODEM   A transfer protocol that defines how computers can send files to each other. Contains the capability to automatically correct errors, pick up where it left off if a connection is broken temporarily, and automatically send the file name.

Index